PESAH READER

ARTICLES WITH INSIGHTS ON PESAH AND THE SEDER

INCLUDING LAWS OF PESAH

Pesah Reader

For more information please contact:
Tebah Educational Services Inc.
by email at info@tebah.org.

Please send your donations (tax-deductible) to:
Tebah Educational Services
34 West 33rd Street, 2nd Floor
New York, NY 10001

Compiled by Nathan M. Dweck

Cover artwork by Moses N. Sutton

ISBN: 978-0-9824875-1-8

Price: $14.95

TEBAH'S HOLIDAY READER SERIES:

HIGH HOLIDAYS READER

PESAH READER

PURIM READER

ROSH HASHANAH READER

SHABUOT READER

SUKKOT READER

TISHA BE'AB READER

YOM KIPPUR READER

We gratefully acknowledge the following permissions:

Rabbi Norman Lamm for 'On Influencing the Future' © 1964

Eliner Library at the Department for Jewish Zionist Education, The Jewish Agency for Israel for Nehama Leibowitz's 'Come Let Us Deal Shrewdly With Them' from 'New Studies in Shemot' © 1976.

The David Cardozo Academy for 'To Be a Matzah' by Rabbi Nathan Lopes Cardozo © 2008

Chiefrabbi.org for 'Miracles' by Rabbi Sir Jonathan Sacks © 2010

Sephardic Institute for 'Halakhot of Pesah' and 'Reflections on Passover' by Rabbi Moshe Shamah © 2010

The Student Organization of Yeshiva for 'The Nine Aspects of the Haggada' by Rabbi Joseph B. Soloveitchik, reprinted from 'The Yeshiva University Haggada', © 1985.

Merkaz Moreshet Israel for 'Pesah – Encourage Questioning' by Rabbi Ralph Tawil

Dedicated in Honor of
Our Loving Parents

Abe and Barbara Franco

From their Children & Grandchildren

Dedicated
In Memory of

Albert Rahmey

By his loving family

SPONSORS:

JACK H. ASHKENAZIE FOUNDATION

MORRIS BENUN

HAROLD DWECK

DR. EDDIE GINDI

RONNY HERSH

ABIE MALEH

SAMMY SUTTON

Tebah Educational Services was founded with the recognition that present-day Judaism requires a greater focus on elucidating the intended meaning of the Biblical text as well as the values and guidelines for living that arise from a more complete understanding of it. Tebah's function is to develop, facilitate and publish various types of educational material, as well as school curricula that promote this goal.

Tebah Executive Committee

Publishing Committee
Eddie A. Ashkenazie * Nathan M. Dweck

Norman E. Greenberg * Moses N. Sutton

Tebah Executive Committee
Eli Benun * Abie Betesh

Morris N. Dweck * Nathan M. Dweck

Eli D. Greenberg Esq. * Ricky Novick

Dr. Morris Shamah

Email: info@tebah.org

Internet: www.tebah.org

Table of Contents

About the Authors

Rabbi Hayyim Angel is the Rabbi of Congregation Shearith Israel on Manhattan's Upper West Side (the Spanish and Portuguese Synagogue). Rabbi Angel currently teaches at Yeshiva University. Email: Rabbi.hjangel@shearithisrael.org; Website: www.shearithisrael.org

Rabbi Nathan Lopes Cardozo, dean of the David Cardozo Institute in Israel, is a prominent lecturer and prolific author who is world renowned for his highly original insights into Judaism. He holds a PhD in Philosophy. Website: www.cardozoschool.org.

Rabbi Yitzchak Etshalom attended Yeshivot Kerem b'Yavne, RIETS and Har Etzion before receiving his S'mikhah from the Chief Rabbinate of Jerusalem. He has been a dynamic educator in the Los Angeles area since returning there in 1985 and has been teaching on the internet since 1994. His first book, *Between The Lines of the Bible* was published by Yashar Books in 2006; volume 2 is expected out in 2010. He currently lives with his wife and 5 children in Los Angeles. Email: rebyitz@gmail.com; Websites: www.etshalom.com & www.dafyomiyicc.org

Rabbi Raymond Harari has been the Rabbi of Congregation Kol Israel, in Brooklyn, NY, since 1998. He received his Semikha from Yeshiva University in 1979. He also received a Masters Degree in Jewish Philosophy from Bernard Revel in 1979, and his PhD in Judaic Studies from New York University in 1995. He is the Head of School at Yeshivah of Flatbush High School. Website: www.kolisrael.org.

Rabbi Alex Israel is a beloved Tanach lecturer and Rebbe, teaching at Jerusalem's finest Yeshivot and Midrashot. Educated at the London School of Economics and Yeshivat Har Etzion, he has published over 150 Tanach articles online. Rav Israel brings the Tanach to life in his popular Israel tours, and volunteers for Tzohar Rabbinic organization, bridging the gap between the religious and secular in Israel. Email: alexisrael99@gmail.com

Rabbi Ezra Labaton has been the Rabbi of Congregation Magen David of West Deal for 28 years. He received his *semikha* from Rabbi J.B. Soloveitchik at Yeshiva University. He has completed his PhD thesis at Brandeis University in the field of biblical exegesis. He was a long-time student of Professor Nahum Sarna, who is recognized as one the world's leading Bible scholars. Website: www.merkaz.com/labaton.htm

Rabbi Norman Lamm is the Rosh Yeshiba of R. Isaac Elchanan Theological Seminary and Chancellor of Yeshiva University. He received a doctorate in the 1960s in Jewish Philosophy at the Bernard Revel Graduate School of Jewish Studies. Email: nlamm@yu.edu. Website: www.yu.edu/lammheritage

Nehama Leibowitz a"h was a noted Israeli biblical scholar and commentator. A long-time professor of Bible at Tel Aviv University, she had an international following of thousands through her weekly parasha sheets. She received a doctorate from the University of Berlin in 1930. Website: http://www.jafi.org.il/education/torani/Nehama

Rabbi Sir Jonathan Henry Sacks has been Chief Rabbi of the United Kingdom since 1991. From 1984-1990 he served as principal of Jews' College. He received a PhD from Oxford University in Philosophy. In 2005 he was knighted by the queen of England. Website: www.chiefrabbi.org

Rabbi Moshe Shamah founded the Sephardic Institute in 1968 and continues as its director. He also serves as head rabbi of Sephardic Synagogue in Brooklyn, NY. Email: mshamah@jseminar.org; Website: www.judaic.org

Rabbi Dr. Moshe Sokolow is the Fanya Gottesfeld Heller Professor of Jewish Education and Associate Dean at the Azrieli Graduate School of Jewish Education and Administration of Yeshiva University. Email: msokolow@yu.edu

Rabbi Joseph Ber Soloveitchik z"l was an American Orthodox rabbi, Talmudist and modern Jewish philosopher. As Rosh Yeshiva of Rabbi Isaac Elchanan Theological Seminary at Yeshiva University in New York City, The Rav, as he came to be known, ordained close to 2,000 rabbis over the course of almost half a century. Website: www.yutorah.org

Rabbi Ralph Tawil received degrees from Columbia University and Yeshiva University and is a Jerusalem Fellow. He was the principal of the Hillel High School in Deal, NJ. He currently lives and teaches in Israel. Email: rtawil@bezeqint.net, Website: http://judaic.org/tabletalk/1tabletalk.html

Halakhot of Pesah[1]

Rabbi Moshe Shamah

I. The Month of Nissan

Although in counting years we begin from Rosh Hashanah – the first of Tishri, the seventh month – the Torah counts months from Nissan, to highlight the Exodus from Egypt, which occurred in that month. Since most of Nissan's days are festive occasions (the first twelve days commemorate the dedication of the Mishkan followed by Pesah), the whole month assumes a festive character; accordingly, *tahanun* supplications (*anna*) are omitted from prayers the entire month. The two Psalms normally recited in the latter portion of *shahrit* that allude to a 'day of distress' (*Ya'ancha* and *Tefilla Ledavi*d) are also omitted when *anna* is omitted.

When one sees two blossoming fruit trees during Nissan, *Birkat Ha'ilanot* is recited. This berakha is recited only once each year by men and women. It may be recited on Shabbat or yom tob. Although Nissan is the proper time for it, it may be recited afterwards but not subsequent to the blossoming stage, when the fruit are growing.

Eulogies are not permitted during Nissan. When appropriate, a short appreciation of the departed with moral instruction is permitted.

II. Searching for Hametz

As the Torah prohibits possession of hametz on Pesah, it is mandatory to check one's home and remove all hametz before Pesah. Despite the fact that the home was thoroughly cleansed of hametz beforehand, on the night

---

[1] In matters of varying customs, these Halakhot follow the general Sephardic custom of the Aleppo-derived communities.

1

before Pesah we perform *bediqat hametz* in all places where it might be found. When Pesah falls on Saturday night, the search is done the Thursday night before.

Before beginning the search, the head of household (the leader of the search) recites the berakha *Asher qideshanu bemisvotav vesivanu 'al bi'ur hames* ("Who has sanctified us with his commandments, and commanded us on the removal of hametz"), which covers the entire process of the removal of hametz from ones property, completed the following morning; no berakha is recited upon the actual removal of the hametz in the morning. After the berakha, one must be careful not to speak until at least beginning the search, so as not interrupt between the berakha and the act for which the berakha was recited. It is proper to refrain from extraneous talk and digressions throughout the search so that it is done correctly. In addition to homes, places of business and cars require checking if hametz is normally brought into them.

Traditionally, the search has been performed by the light of a single wick candle (a multi-wick one is dangerous). Today, because of safety reasons and superior effectiveness in searching, a flashlight is preferable. A widespread custom is to use a candle for the first moments of the search for symbolic reasons and then switch to a flashlight. The berakha is recited even if one uses only a flashlight.

As the home is usually thoroughly cleansed from hametz before the *bediqah*, it is customary but not mandatory to place pieces of hametz where the searcher will surely find them so that he will have hametz to burn. Immediately after the search at night, the owner should recite *Bitul Hames*, an annulment/renunciation of hametz in his possession. As most people will continue owning and benefiting from hametz until the morning, this first *bitul* is directed only to hametz that the owner does not know about. One should understand what he is saying. If one

2

does not understand the traditional Aramaic words of the *bitul* formula (found at the beginning of the Hagaddah or Mahzor), he should recite it in English. Translations are readily available.

If one embarks on a journey within 30 days before Pesah and no one remains at home to do *bediqah* at the designated time, it should be done before leaving without reciting the berakha. When one closes his home prior to the evening of *bediqat hametz* and intends to be away the entire holiday, such as when a family goes out of town, if he sells any and all hametz in his home, he does not have to search it. He searches his hotel room and makes bitul for any hametz that may remain in his possession. The same applies to a second home that remains closed for the duration of the holiday. One who plans to leave the day of Ereb Pesah, since he is still at home at the time of *bediqat hametz*, is required to perform it.

One who was planning to be away all Pesah and sold the hametz in his home without making *bediqah* but unexpectedly returned must search for and gather the sold hametz that was not put away and place it in a closed off or out of the way location, to prevent someone inadvertently partaking of it.

III. Ereb Pesah

It is forbidden to eat hametz after the fourth hour of the day beginning from dawn. These hours are calculated according to a system whereby dawn to dusk is divided into twelve hours regardless of the actual length of that particular day (*sha'ot zemaniyot*/proportional hours). The time will vary slightly each year according to the solar date on which Pesah occurs, but generally it is about 8:45 a.m. E.S.T.[2] Consult the specific schedule for that year for exact times.

---

[2] Following times in New York.

The prohibition to benefit from hametz, which includes selling it, begins one proportional hour after the deadline for eating, generally about 10:00 a.m. E.S.T. It is preferable to completely get rid of all hametz without having to sell. However, selling is permitted even if the hametz remains in the overall confines of one's home, providing the hametz's specific location is also sold or leased to the non-Jew. As this transaction must be done legally, it is advisable for one who sells hametz that is going to remain in the overall confines of his property to do so through a rabbi. Hametz being sold should be gathered together, covered and placed where no member of the household would forget and mistakenly partake of it.

The destruction of any remaining hametz should be done before the end of the fifth hour. It may be accomplished either by burning, shredding, dissolving, etc. It is customary and preferable to destroy hametz through burning. When Ereb Pesah falls on Shabbat, the burning takes place on Friday.

Hametz in a garbage receptacle placed by the street curb in front of one's home is *hefker* (ownership is relinquished) and not in one's possession even if the sanitation department did not remove it by the end of the fifth hour. It is preferable that the hametz not be in one's private receptacle but in a carton or bag that will be collected with the hametz.

After getting rid of all hametz, one recites *Bitul Hames* again. This second recitation, unlike the night before, includes all hametz one owns. Selling hametz to a non-Jew should be done before this bitul, since hametz being sold is not that which is being annulled or renounced.

Matzah should not be eaten Ereb Pesah even in the morning so as to eat the matzah of the Seder with greater desire and appetite. This applies only to matzah with which one may fulfill the obligation in the evening, not egg

4

matzah which is called 'rich' matzah and is unsuitable for fulfilling the *mitzvah*.

Cake made with matzah meal, since it is baked the way bread or matzah is, should also not be eaten Ereb Pesah. Although the matzah meal was mixed with 'enriching' items, the mixing was done after the matzah received its identity as matzah fit for the mitzvah of the Seder, not at the original kneading like egg matzah. On the other hand, if the matzah is not baked but fried or cooked, such as *i'jeh masso* (matzah fried in oil with eggs), it is permitted Ereb Pesah.

One should not eat a filling meal of any food in the later afternoon as it may lessen one's appetite for the evening's matzah.

There is a custom for first born males to fast Ereb Pesah as a sign of appreciation for the Almighty's sparing Israel's first-born when smiting the Egyptian first-born. This fast is overridden if the first-born participates in a *se'udat misvah* (festive meal attached to a mitzvah), including the completion of a tractate of the Talmud even though he himself has not learned that tractate.

IV. Shabbat Ereb Pesah (following times in New York)

1. The *Siyyum Bekhorot* is pushed back to Thursday and is treated more leniently than in other years. A non-bekhor father who might normally attend a siyyum on behalf of his first born minor son is exempt, as are women *bekhorot*.

2. *Bediqat Hames* (searching for hametz) is done Thursday night after the stars appear (approximately 25 minutes after sunset [for the conclusion of Shabbat we wait 35 minutes]) followed by recital of the first *Kal Hamirah* (annulling unseen hametz).

3. Hametz is burned Friday morning by the end of the fifth hour (usually approximately 10:00 a.m.), the same time as

in other years so that there be one uniform halakha for all years, notwithstanding that this year we are permitted to eat and own hametz until Shabbat morning.

4. The second *Kal Hamirah* (annulling all hametz) is recited Shabbat morning by the end of the fifth hour (usually approximately 10:00 a.m.).

5. Regarding *Hamosi* and Birkat Hamazon for the meals of Friday night and Shabbat day, several options are available:

A. We may eat bread (preferably pita which produces fewer crumbs) Friday night and Shabbat morning until the end of the fourth hour (usually approximately 8:45 a.m.), taking care not to have hametz spread over the house or fall on Pesah utensils. Only a minimal amount of hametz, that which is expected to be eaten, should be left for this purpose. Any leftover hametz must be discarded by 10:00 a.m., by which time the final *Kal Hamirah* is recited. Disposal of hametz should be into a garbage bag or receptacle left outside the home within the home's erub area (halakhic enclosure for purposes of carrying on Shabbat.) As a last resort hametz leftovers may be flushed away. This option generally involves attending first minyan that Shabbat morning.

B. One who chooses to remove all hametz on Friday, reciting the final *Kal Hamira* at that time, and uses regular matzah Friday night in place of bread, would recite *Hamosi* and Birkat Hamazon as during Pesah. For the Shabbat day meal, fried or cooked whole matzah, prepared from before Shabbat, may be used. The blessings on these items would be as during Pesah: *Hamosi* and Birkat Hamazon. Although we may not eat regular matzah on Ereb Pesah Shabbat during the daytime, fried or cooked matzah is allowed.

C. Egg Matzah is Mezonot unless one eats a large amount of it (at least 6 ounces), in which case *Hamosi* and Birkat Hamazon are recited.

V. Hametz

The Torah forbids eating, deriving benefit from, or owning hametz during Pesah. Hametz results when any of the five grains (wheat, barley, rye, oats, spelt), after harvesting, makes contact with water and fermentation takes place. Mixtures including hametz are also prohibited as are edible extracts and alcoholic fermentation of hametz. Bread, cereal, cake, cookies, crackers, pastas and spaghetti from the five grains are pure hametz.

Rice, soy, corn (maize), potatoes, fruits, vegetables, meat, poultry, fish and dairy products are permitted when in their pure form. If processed, one must be careful that the product does not include or did not absorb from a hametz derivative.

Hametz derivatives unfit for human or animal consumption are not considered food and are permitted on Pesah. This includes virtually all deodorants, soaps, cleansers and cleaning agents, polishes, toothpastes, lipsticks, most cosmetics and medicines (all ill tasting liquids, tablets and capsules), etc.

Hametz mixed into non-hametz substances during Pesah is not annulled in the manner that prohibited food items are annulled all year long, such as mixtures of one in sixty. Perhaps more than any other, it is this halakha that requires an extra measure of care with food throughout Pesah.

However, hametz that was mixed with non-hametz is annulled before Pesah in the standard manner and remains annulled during Pesah. This principle applies even if inclusion of the hametz ingredient was not known before Pesah. Thus, foods prepared before Pesah that are known to be kosher all year long, that do not have hametz as an ingredient, even were they somehow to have a minor amount of hametz mixed in and annulled before Pesah, are acceptable during Pesah. Such foods do not necessarily require special supervision. Included in this category are canned, frozen and most dried fruits and vegetables, fruit juices, sugar, salt, plain tea, plain potato chips, pure coffees, pure chocolates, pure vegetable oils, tomato sauce, milk, butter and plain dairy products.

Based on this halakha, many homemakers bake, cook and purchase as much as possible of their Pesah needs before the onset of the holiday.

If hametz gets mixed into food even during Pesah, and gives a negative taste into the food, that food is permitted. Thus, if Pesah food was mistakenly cooked in clean non-Pesah utensils that weren't used for 24 hours, the food is permitted. This is based on the principle that whatever is absorbed in the walls of utensils gives a spoiled taste after 24 hours.

Ashkenazim eating by Sephardim during Passover need not be concerned that the vessels in which foods were prepared were also used for rice and legumes, which most Ashkenazim do not eat during Pesah. The Ashkenazic strictness on these items is an extreme cautionary measure and does not carry over to vessels.[3]

One who finds hametz in his possession during hol hamo'ed should burn it immediately; if found on yom tob, however, it should be covered until after yom tob, at which time it should be burned. There is no berakha on these cases of burning.

Hametz be'ayin (roughly translated "visible," not a mixture) which was in the possession of a Jew during Pesah is prohibited even after Pesah.

---

[3] See Hakham Ovadia Yosef, *Yehave Da'at* 5:32.

VI. Matzah

It is a Biblical command to eat matzah (unleavened bread) on the first night of Pesah. It commemorates our ancestors not having time to allow their dough to leaven before baking, as they were chased out of Egypt. Also, matzah is the "bread of affliction," recalling the slavery.

Matzah is made from flour of one of the five types of grains that can become hametz, kneaded with water and baked before it has a chance to begin leavening (rising). For this *mitzvah* one should obtain matzah that has been under supervision that it did not come into contact with water from the grain harvest. Each person should eat at least the *kazzayit* for *hamosi*, but preferably all matzah for the mitzvot required at the Seder, from such matzah. If not available, matzah under supervision from the grinding is sufficient. All commercial Passover matzah from the companies displaying supervision today has been "watched" at least from the time of grinding.

Matzah, once baked, may be dipped in water. An elderly or ill person may fulfill the *mitzvah* in such a manner.

Egg matzah is permitted to be eaten during Pesah. Indeed, matzah which was kneaded with fruit juice and not water, which is the standard procedure for making egg matzah, does not become hametz even if the dough was left unbaked for a lengthy period of time. (The acid does not permit activation of the leavening enzyme in the dough.) However, egg matzah is not "poor man's bread" and cannot be used to fulfill the obligations of the Seder.

The berakha on regular matzah during all of Pesah is *hamosi* even if one is eating a very small amount. During Pesah, matzah is our bread. Even when regular matzah is fried or cooked during Pesah, such as in *i'jeh masso* or *kibbeh masso* (another matzah delicacy), its berakha is *hamosi*. All year long many Sephardim recite mezonot on regular matzah except when one is *qobeya' se'uda* (there are various opinions here, essentially when one uses matzah to get full as bread) as matzah is normally a snack food in the category of a cracker. The berakha *Al Akhilat Masah* is added to *hamosi* only at the Seder. Egg matzah, even during Pesah, is mezonot (except if one is *qobeya' se'uda*).

VII. Utensils for Passover

Pesah requires special utensils to ensure that even a little hametz not enter our food.

Glassware does not absorb and merely requires washing to be kosher for Pesah. This includes Duralex, Pyrex, Corningware, Corelle and colored glass.

Absorption by utensils from food takes place in the presence of heat; thus, utensils that come into contact with foods and liquids that generally are not hot (salad bowls, fruit trays, refrigerator trays, can openers, etc.) can be used on Pesah after being washed. The same applies to tabletops and counters.

Utensils used with heat but known not to be used for hametz all year long are acceptable for Pesah, such as teapots, hot water urns and decanters.

Koshering utensils is according to its general use. As the utensil absorbed so will it emit what it absorbed. Hametz pots and pans, flatware, blenders, etc. made of metal, wood, rubber, stone, bone or plastic (including melmac and tupperware), can be made usable for Pesah by *hag'alah*.

Hag'alah is total submersion of the item being koshered into a large pot of boiling water for several seconds. If the item cannot fit completely into a large pot, it may be submersed portion by portion. The utensils must be cleaned before immersion.

If one is to make *hag'alah*, it is preferable to do so before Pesah. However, it can be made during hol hamo'ed

10

providing the hametz utensil being cleaned was not used for 24 hours, based on the principle that whatever is absorbed in a utensil's walls emits a spoiled taste after 24 hours.

When *hag'alah* is made on items that had not been used for 24 hours in a pot that also had not been used for 24 hours, it does not matter if the items or pot are dairy or meat, or if the pot is hametz or kosher for Passover.

Metals used directly on the fire with hametz require *liboon* (placement on fire until red hot).

Utensils usually used for cold substances that on occasion were used for hot hametz, such as metal cold liquid drinking cups, are treated according to their usual use and merely require washing (after 24 hours from hametz use). Although the vessel on occasion definitely absorbed hametz, after 24 hours whatever was absorbed is spoiled; thus there is no possibility of a Torah infraction and the rabbis did not decree a prohibition when the usage with heat was not according to the vessel's standard usage.

Hametz earthenware utensils cannot be made usable for Passover. Glazed chinaware is very different from classic earthenware and many authorities permit koshering such utensils through *hag'alah* or pouring boiling water on them. An Orthodox rabbi should be consulted regarding the specific type of chinaware in question.

Porcelain, enamel and steel sinks are koshered by pouring boiling water all around their receptacle portion.

Ovens and their racks should be cleansed for Passover as follows: after thoroughly cleaning with a scouring agent, leave unused for 24 hours; then heat at maximum for an hour. Self cleaning ovens merely need to be run through a self cleaning cycle. In the case of microwave ovens, after cleaning, insert a microwave safe utensil with water and microwave at maximum for several minutes, until the oven fills with steam.

Dishwashers are koshered by their normal use of boiling water and soap. Tablecloths are koshered by washing in soap and water.

VIII. The Seder

Qadesh: After arranging the items on the Seder table correctly, the head of household recites *qiddush*. Everyone should be standing and attentive and there should be no talking during the recital of the berakhot. *Qiddush* is recited after *set hakokhabim* (the appearance of stars, which in New York is about 35 minutes after sunset).

Each person should have his or her own cup containing at least 3 ounces (*rebi'it*) of wine and drink at least the majority of the cup. Red wine is preferable but grape juice may be used. This is the first of the four Seder cups. These regulations apply to all four cups. The berakha of *hagefen* is recited on the first and third cups only. The drinking of the four cups and the eating of the matzot are done while reclining to the left. A left-handed person also reclines to the left.

Urhas: Each person washes his or her hands for the wet vegetables going to be eaten next. A berakha is not recited on this washing of hands.

Karpas: We eat less than a *kazzayit* of a green vegetable (celery is our custom) after dipping it in salt water. [The reason for having less than a *kazzayit* is to avoid a centuries old unresolved question: should one who eats a measure that requires *berakha aharona* of *Bore Nefashot* recite that berakha if he plans to shortly afterwards recite *hamosi* that will eventually be followed by Birkat Hamazon? We try to avoid omitting a required berakha but not to recite an unrequired berakha.]

We recite *Boreh Peri Ha'adamah* on the karpas vegetable. It is our custom to have intention that this berakha "cover" the *adamah* of the maror, which will be eaten later. Although the maror will be eaten after *hamosi*,

12

it is necessarily eaten alone and perhaps not covered by *hamosi*. So again, to avoid a question we cover it with the berakha on the karpas.

Yahas: The middle matzah is broken, by hand, into two pieces. The smaller piece is replaced between the two whole matzot while the larger piece is set aside for Afiqoman. Each individual takes a turn carrying the afiqoman matzah, wrapped in a cloth holder, over one's shoulder reciting *Mish'arotam...* as a symbolic reenactment of the Exodus.

Magid: One raises the matzah and recites *Keha Lahma 'Anya*. The tray is removed for children to question, the second cup of wine is poured, *Ma Nishtana* is recited, the tray returned, and the matzot uncovered. The Haggadah is read with great joy. Questions are asked, explanations are given. The relating by fathers to sons of the Exodus from Egypt and the Almighty's miracles is the central theme of the Seder. Those who do not understand Hebrew must perform this *mitzvah* in a language they understand. English translations are readily available.

Rohsa: One should wash his or her hands and recite the berakha *'Al Netilat Yadayim* to prepare for *hamosi*.

Mosi Masah: The head of the household raises all 3 matzot (the two whole and one broken) and recites the berakha of *hamosi*. Next, he releases the bottom whole matzah and recites the berakha of *Al Akhilat Masah*. Reclining to their left, all eat at least one *kazzayit* (approximately one ounce). It is preferable to eat two *kazzaytim*, one for *Mosi* and one for *Masah*. At least one *kazzayit* should be eaten within a four minute period to be considered a single eating.

Maror: *Kazzayit* maror (bitter herbs) is dipped in haroset (a date, nut and wine mixture), the berakha *Al Akhilat Maror* is recited, and the maror is eaten without reclining. Romaine Lettuce is a preferred vegetable for maror but great care must be taken that it first be thoroughly checked and cleansed of any tiny insects that are often found in it. Escarole or endives are acceptable and generally easier to check.

Korekh: A sandwich containing one *kazzayit* each of matzah and maror is dipped in haroset and eaten in a reclining position after reciting the explanation of this custom, *Zekher Lamiqdash* etc. Those for whom it is difficult to have *kazzayit* matzah and maror may eat smaller measures for korekh.

Shulhan Orekh: The egg and shankbone are eaten followed by the meal. On the egg we recite *Zekher LeQorban Hagiga*. Nothing is recited on the shankbone. To distinguish from the Pesah sacrifice brought in the days of the Bet Hamiqdash which was only broiled, the shankbone should also be cooked. It is important not to be totally satiated during the meal in order to leave room for the afiqoman, which must be eaten "with appetite."

Safoon: After the meal a piece of the middle matzah is distributed to each person, to which additional matzah is added to make a *kazzayit*. This should be eaten reclining before midnight.

Barekh: The third cup of wine is poured and Birkat Hamazon is recited.

Hallel: Hagefen is recited before drinking the third cup, reclining. One should have intention to also cover the fourth cup with this berakha. The remainder of Hallel is recited without a berakha beforehand, followed by Nishmat and the concluding berakha of Hallel. The fourth cup is drunk, reclining, followed by *berakha aharona*.

Nirsa: It is customary to sing and continue discussion of the Exodus and other miracles that the Almighty wrought until one falls asleep.

IX. Measurements

The measure for a *kazzayit* matzah is thought by many in our community to be one ounce of weight. However, the original measure of a *kazzayit* (meaning an olive) is basically a volume one, widely interpreted as 1/2 the volume of an average egg. (Although the olive was widely cited by the rabbis of old, it was supplanted by the egg for actual measurements.) The egg used for determining this measure must be an average one of the present time and locale. The weight measure we use today was derived from the volume; rabbis of the past calculated the volume and then weighed it for the convenience of the public.

A question has arisen with the one ounce of weight measure. An average to large size egg of today displaces approximately two fluid ounces. The cubic volume of one fluid ounce can be completely filled with less than 2/3 of an ounce (weight) of matzah. Thus, when eating the *mosi masah*, where it is preferable to eat two *kazzaytim*, one who is unable to eat two ounces may eat 1.33 ounces for two *kazzaytim*. Of course, as stated earlier, *bedi'abad* one *kazzayit* is sufficient.

The measure for a *rebi'it* wine is (just under) three fluid ounces. This is based on the Talmudic standard that a *rebi'it* is the displacement of 1.5 eggs and on the fact that an average egg today displaces approximately two fluid ounces.

A *kazzayit* karpas or maror is of lesser weight than a *kazzayit* matzah as vegetables have a lower density of mass and thus a lower weight for the standard volume of half an egg's displacement.

X. Prayers

Each day of Pesah before arbit and during *shahrit*, we recite Psalm 107 which deals with various situations from which the psalmist was redeemed. The Pesah redemption is closely identified with all redemptions of the Almighty.

Ya'ale veyabo is recited in each amida. If it was omitted during hol hamo'ed one repeats the amida. During yom tob it depends if mention of Pesah was made independently of it or not. *Ya'ale veyabo* is also recited in Birkat Hamazon during Pesah.

After the amida of arbit the first two nights, complete Hallel is recited with berakhot.

Hallel is recited after the amida of *shahrit* each day. On the first two days the berakhot before and after are recited; on the latter days not. One explanation for the difference with Sukkot when we recite Hallel each day with berakhot is that the latter days of Pesah commemorate the drowning of the Egyptians at the Red Sea. The Midrash describes it as if the Almighty said to the heavenly angels: "My creatures (the Egyptians) are drowning and you are singing?" So we tone down the Hallel recital by skipping parts (thus not saying the berakhot).

Specified Pesah selections are read from the Torah each morning. The minimum number of aliyot on yom tob is five plus maftir. The number of aliyot on hol hamo'ed is four. Even on hol hamo'ed two *Sifre Torah* are taken out each day.

Musaf prayer is recited daily. We begin reciting *Morid Hatal* during Musaf of the first day and *Barekhenu* during the first weekday arbit of hol hamo'ed. Tefillin are not donned during the days of Pesah.

Our Journey in the Haggadah: How Its Narratives and Observances Enable Us to Experience the Exodus

Rabbi Hayyim Angel

I. Introduction

Though many read the Haggadah as a unified text, it was not composed at one time by a single author. Rather, it is a compilation of biblical, talmudic and midrashic texts, with several other passages that were added over the centuries.[1] Despite its composite nature, the Haggadah in its current form may be understood as containing a fairly coherent structure. It creates a collective effect that enables us to understand and experience the journey of our ancestors. As the Haggadah exhorts us, we must consider ourselves as though we left Egypt, actively identifying with our past rather than merely recounting ancient history. The Exodus lies at the root of our eternal covenantal relationship with God.

---

[1] Shemuel & Ze'ev Safrai write that most of the core of our Haggadah, including the Kiddush, the Four Questions, the Four Children, the midrashic readings, Rabban Gamliel, the blessing at the end of *maggid* originated in the time of the Mishnah and were set by the 9th century. "This is the bread of affliction" (*ha lahma anya*) and "In each generation" (*be-khol dor va-dor*) hail from the 9th-10th centuries. Components such as the story of the five rabbis at B'nei B'rak and R. Elazar; the Midrash about the number of plagues at the Red Sea; Hallel HaGadol and Nishmat; all existed as earlier texts before their incorporation into the Haggadah. "Pour out Your wrath" (*shefokh hamatekha*) and the custom of hiding the *afikoman* are later additions. All of the above was set by 11th century. The only significant additions after the 11th century are the songs at the end (*Haggadat Hazal* [Jerusalem: Karta, 1998], pp. 70-71).

17

The essential aspects of the Passover story are not taken from the primary account in the book of Exodus. Rather, they derive from other biblical texts and later rabbinic sources. The Haggadah expects that we have learned the book of Exodus and laws of Passover as well.

The Haggadah merges laws with narrative. Its text and symbols take us on a journey that begins with freedom, then a descent into slavery, to the Exodus, and on into the messianic age. Though we may feel free today, we are in exile so long as the Temple is not rebuilt. Many of our Seder observances remind us of the Temple and our prayer for its rebuilding.

The Haggadah also presents a strong educational agenda. Although most traditions are passed from the older generation to the younger, the older generation must be open to learning from the younger. Often, it is their innocent questions that remind us of how much we still must learn and explore.

In this essay, we will use the foregoing axioms to outline the journey of the Haggadah in its current form, using the text and translation of Rabbi Marc D. Angel's *A Sephardic Passover Haggadah*.[2] This study is not an attempt to uncover the original meaning of the Passover symbols or why certain passages were incorporated into the Haggadah. However, perhaps we will approach the inner logic of our current version of the Haggadah and its symbols as they came to be traditionally understood.

II. The First Four Stages: From Freedom Into Slavery

Kadesh: Wine symbolizes festivity and happiness. Kiddush represents our sanctification of time, another sign of freedom.[3] We recline as we drink the wine, a sign of

---

[2] *A Sephardic Passover Haggadah*, with translation and commentary prepared by Rabbi Marc D. Angel (Hoboken: KTAV, 1988).
[3] See, for example, Seforno on Ex. 12:2.

freedom from Roman times, when the core observances of the Seder were codified by the rabbis of the Mishnah. Many also have the custom of having others pour the wine for them, yet another symbol of luxury and freedom. Thus, the Haggadah begins by making us feel free and noble.

Rehatz: We ritually wash our hands before dipping the *karpas* vegetable into salt water or vinegar. As with the pouring of the wine, many have the custom for others to wash their hands, symbolizing luxury and freedom. Rabbi Naftali Tzvi Yehudah Berlin (Netziv, 1817-1893, Lithuania) observes that many do not follow this talmudic practice of washing hands before dipping any food into a liquid anymore. Doing so at the Seder serves as a reminder of our practices in Temple times. We thus remain in freedom mode for *rehatz*, but begin to think about the absence of the Temple.

Karpas: Dipping an appetizer is another sign of freedom and nobility from Roman times. However, we dip the vegetable into either salt water or vinegar which came to be understood as symbolic of the tears of slavery. In addition, the technical ritual reason behind eating *karpas* resolves a halakhic debate over whether we are required to make a blessing of *Borei peri ha-adamah* over the Maror later. On the one hand, we eat Maror after Matzah and therefore have already washed and recited *ha-Motzi*. On the other hand, it is unclear that the Maror should be subsumed under the "dinner" covered by the Matzah since it is its own independent mitzvah. Consequently, the *ha-adamah* we recite over the *karpas* absolves us of this doubt, and we are required to keep the Maror in mind for this blessing.[4] In symbolic terms, while we are dipping an appetizer as a sign of freedom and luxury, we experience the tears of slavery, and we think about the Maror, which the Haggadah casts as

---

[4] See *Pesahim* 114b; Shulhan Arukh, *Orah Hayyim* 473:6; 475:2.

a symbol of the bitterness of slavery.[5] Thus, we are beginning our descent into slavery.

Yahatz: The Haggadah identifies two reasons for eating Matzah. One is explicit in the Torah (Ex. 12:39), that our ancestors had to rush out of Egypt during the Exodus. However, the Haggadah introduces another element: the Israelites ate Matzah while yet slaves in Egypt. The Torah's expression *lehem 'oni* (Deut. 16:3; "bread of affliction") lends itself to this midrashic interpretation.

Yahatz focuses exclusively on this slavery aspect of Matzah—poor people break their bread and save some for later, not knowing when they will next receive more food (see *Berakhot* 39b). By this point, then, we have descended into slavery. At the same time, the other half of this Matzah will be used for the *tzafun-afikoman*, which represents the Passover offering, and is part of the freedom part of the Seder. Even as we descend into slavery with our ancestors, the Haggadah provides us with a glimpse of the redemption.

To summarize, *kaddesh* begins with our experiencing freedom and luxury. *Rehatz* also is a sign of freedom, but raises the specter of there no longer being a Temple. *Karpas* continues the trend of freedom but more overtly

---

[5] The symbol of the Maror underwent an evolution. Joseph Tabory notes that during the Roman meal, the dipping of lettuce as a first course was the most common appetizer. By the fourth century, the Talmud ruled that the appetizer must be a different vegetable (*karpas*) so that the Maror could be eaten for the first time as a mitzvah with a blessing (*The JPS Commentary on the Haggadah: Historical Introduction, Translation, and Commentary* [Philadelphia: Jewish Publication Society, 2008], pp. 23-24).

In *Pesahim* 39a, one Sage explains that we use *hasa* (romaine lettuce, the talmudically preferred Maror even though five different vegetables are suitable) since God pitied our ancestors. Another Sage derives additional meaning from the fact that romaine lettuce begins by tasting sweet, but leaves a bitter aftertaste. This sensory process resembles our ancestors' coming to Egypt as nobles and their subsequent enslavement.

gives us a taste of slavery by reminding us of tears and bitterness. *Yahatz* completes the descent into slavery. Even before we begin the *maggid*, then, the Haggadah has enabled us to experience the freedom and nobility of the Patriarchs; the descent to Egypt with Joseph and his brothers; and the enslavement of their descendents.

III. *Maggid*: From Slavery to Freedom

A. Educational Framework

At this point in our journey, we are slaves. We begin the primary component of the Haggadah—the *maggid*—from this state of slavery.

Ha Lahma Anya: We continue to employ the "bread of affliction" imagery of the Matzah, since we are slaves now. This opening passage of *maggid* also connects us to our ancestors: "This is the bread of affliction which our ancestors ate in the land of Egypt...Now we are here enslaved..." The Haggadah is an experience of our journey and connection to our past and our future. While beginning our experience by identifying with the slavery of our ancestors, the passage moves into our own exile and desire for redemption.

Mah Nishtanah–The Four Children: Before continuing our journey, we shift our focus to education. The Haggadah prizes the spirit of questioning. The wise of the four children does not necessarily know more than his less appealing counterparts. His wisdom is found in his questioning: "What are the testimonies, statutes, and laws which the Lord our God has commanded you?" To create a society of wise children, the Haggadah challenges us to explore and live our traditions. Rabbi Barukh Epstein (1860-1941, Lithuania) observes that the opposite of the wicked child is not a *tzaddik*, or "righteous" child. Some might define a righteous person as one who uncritically observes commandments. Therefore, the Haggadah teaches that the ideal wise child asks, challenges, and thinks as he grows in his commitment to the Torah.

Avadim Hayinu: The Haggadah sets the educational agenda for our observances in general: we are not simply recounting ancient history; we are a living part of that memory and connect to our ancestors through an acknowledgement that all later generations are indebted to God for the original Exodus. "If the Holy One blessed be He had not brought out our ancestors from Egypt, we and our children and grandchildren would yet be enslaved to Pharaoh in Egypt."

Ma'aseh Be-Ribbi Eliezer: The five rabbis who stayed up all night in B'nei B'rak inspire us to realize that the more knowledgeable one is the more exciting this learning becomes. These rabbis allowed their conversation to take flight, losing track of time as they experienced the Exodus and actively connected to our texts and traditions.[6] This passage thus venerates our teachers.

Amar Ribbi El'azar: As a complement to the previous paragraph, this passage reminds us that the lesser scholar Ben Zoma had something valuable to teach the greatest Sages of his generation. Learning moves in both directions, and everyone has something important to contribute to the conversation.

Yakhol Me-Rosh Hodesh: The Haggadah again stresses its premium value on the combination of education and experience. "The commandment [to discuss the Exodus from Egypt] applies specifically to the time when Matzah and Maror are set before you." To recount the story of the Exodus meaningfully, we must observe the rituals alongside it.

---

[6] Unlike most other rabbinic passages in the Haggadah which are excerpted from the Talmud and midrashic collections, this paragraph is unattested in rabbinic literature outside the Haggadah. See Joseph Tabory, *JPS Commentary on the Haggadah*, p. 38 for discussion of a parallel in the *Tosefta*.

B. The Journey Resumes

Now that we have established a proper educational framework, we can return to our journey. At the last checkpoint, we were slaves pointing to our bread of affliction, longing for the redemption. The passages employed in this section of the Haggadah each move us a little further ahead in the journey, as we shall see.

Mi-Tehillah Ovedei Avodah Zarah: Following the trend of *maggid*, we begin with the past but immediately shift into the relevance of this discussion to us: "In the beginning our ancestors were idolaters; but now, God has drawn us to His service." We quote from the covenant in the book of Joshua:

> In olden times, your forefathers—Terah, father of Abraham and father of Nahor—lived beyond the Euphrates and worshiped other gods. But I took your father Abraham from beyond the Euphrates and led him through the whole land of Canaan and multiplied his offspring. I gave him Isaac, and to Isaac I gave Jacob and Esau. I gave Esau the hill country of Seir as his possession, while Jacob and his children went down to Egypt (Josh. 24:2-4).[7]

Beginning the story with our idolatrous origins is humbling, and this historical review also helps us appreciate our service of God by not taking it for granted. However, the Haggadah cuts the story line of this chapter in Joshua. The very next verses in the book of Joshua read:

> Then I sent Moses and Aaron, and I plagued Egypt with [the wonders] that I wrought in their midst, after which I freed you—I freed your fathers—from Egypt, and you came to the Sea. But the Egyptians pursued your fathers

---

[7] Translations of biblical passages are taken from the New Jewish Publication Society *Tanakh* (Philadelphia, 1985).

to the Sea of Reeds with chariots and horsemen. They cried out to the LORD, and He put darkness between you and the Egyptians; then He brought the Sea upon them, and it covered them. Your own eyes saw what I did to the Egyptians (Josh. 24:5-7).

Given the direct relevance of these verses to the Passover story, why are they not included in the Haggadah? It appears that the Haggadah does not cite these verses because we are not yet up to that stage in our journey. The Haggadah thus far has brought us only to Egypt.

Hi She-Amedah: The Haggadah again affirms the connection between our ancestors and our contemporary lives. "This promise has held true for our ancestors and for us. Not only one enemy has risen against us; but in every generation enemies rise against us to destroy us. And the Holy One, blessed be He, saves us from their hand." The slavery and Exodus thereby become a paradigm for all later history.

Tzei Ve-Lammed: The midrashic expansion is based on Deuteronomy 26, the confession that a farmer would make upon bringing his first fruits:

My father was a fugitive Aramean. He went down to Egypt with meager numbers and sojourned there; but there he became a great and very populous nation. The Egyptians dealt harshly with us and oppressed us; they imposed heavy labor upon us. We cried to the LORD, the God of our fathers, and the LORD heard our plea and saw our plight, our misery, and our oppression. The LORD freed us from Egypt by a mighty hand, by an outstretched arm and awesome power, and by signs and portents (Deut. 26:5-8).

We thus continue our journey having arrived in Egypt, from where the passage in Joshua had left off. Through a midrashic discussion of the biblical verses, we travel from Jacob's descent into Egypt, to the growth of the family into a nation, to the slavery, and then on through the plagues and Exodus. By the end of this passage, we have been redeemed from Egypt.

As with the passage from Joshua 24, the Haggadah once again cuts off this biblical passage before the end of its story. The next verse reads:

> He brought us to this place and gave us this land, a land flowing with milk and honey (Deut. 26:9).

In Temple times, Jews evidently did read that next verse (see Mishnah *Pesahim* 10:4).[8] However, the conceptual value of stopping the story is consistent with our experience in the Haggadah. This biblical passage as employed by our Haggadah takes us up through our ancestors' exodus from Egypt, so we have not yet arrived in the land of Israel.

Ribbi Yosei Ha-Gelili Omer–Dayyenu: After enumerating the plagues, the Haggadah quotes from *Midrash Tehillim* 78, where Sages successively suggest that there were 50, 200, or even 250 plagues at the Red Sea. Psalm 78 is primarily concerned with God's benevolent acts towards Israel, coupled with Israel's ingratitude. Psalm 78 attempts to inspire later generations not to be like their ancestors in this ingratitude:

> He established a decree in Jacob, ordained a teaching in Israel, charging our fathers to make them known to their children, that a future generation might know—children yet to be born—and in turn tell their children that they might put their confidence in God, and not forget God's great deeds, but observe His commandments, and not be like their fathers, a wayward and defiant generation, a generation whose heart was inconstant, whose spirit was not true to God (Ps. 78:5).

---

[8] Cf. Joseph Tabory, *JPS Commentary on the Haggadah*, p. 33.

Several Midrashim on this Psalm magnify God's miracles even more than in the accounts in Tanakh, including the passage incorporated in the Haggadah that multiplies the plagues at the Red Sea. From this vantage point, our ancestors were even more ungrateful to God. The Haggadah then follows this excerpt with *dayyenu*, to express profound gratitude over every step of the Exodus process. The juxtaposition of these passages conveys the lesson that the Psalmist and the midrashic expansions wanted us to learn.

In addition to expressing proper gratitude for God's goodness, *dayyenu* carries our journey forward. It picks up with the plagues and Exodus—precisely where the passage we read from Deuteronomy 26 had left us off. It then takes us ahead to the reception of the Torah at Sinai, to the land of Israel, and finally to the Temple: "He gave us the Torah, He led us into the land of Israel, and He built for us the chosen Temple to atone for our sins."

Rabban Gamliel Hayah Omer: Now that we are in the land of Israel and standing at the Temple, we can observe the laws of Passover! We describe the Passover offering during Temple times, Matzah and Maror and their significance. It also is noteworthy that the reason given for eating Matzah is freedom—unlike the slavery section earlier that focused on bread of affliction (*yahatz-ha lahma anya*). "This Matzah which we eat is…because the dough of our ancestors did not have time to leaven before the Holy One blessed be He…redeemed them suddenly."

Be-Khol Dor Va-Dor–Hallel: The primary purpose of the Haggadah is completely spelled out by now. "In each generation a person is obligated to see himself as though he went out of Egypt…For not only did the Holy One blessed be He redeem our ancestors, but He also redeemed us along with them…" Since we have been redeemed along with our ancestors, we recite the first two chapters of the Hallel (Ps. 113-114). These Psalms likewise take us from the Exodus to entry into Israel. R. Judah Loew of Prague (Maharal, c. 1520-1609) explains that we save the other half of Hallel (Ps. 115-118) for after the Grace after Meals, when we pray for our own redemption. Rabbi Joseph Soloveitchik adds that Psalms 113-114 consist of pure praise, befitting an account of the Exodus from Egypt which already has occurred. Psalms 115-118 contain both praise and petition, relevant to our future redemption for which we long.[9]

Asher Ge'alanu: Now that we have completed our journey and have chanted the Hallel thanking God for redeeming us, we conclude *maggid* with a blessing: "You are blessed, Lord our God...Who has redeemed us and redeemed our ancestors from Egypt and has brought us to this night to eat Matzah and Maror..." For the first time in the Haggadah, we place ourselves before our ancestors, since our experience has become primary. As we express gratitude to God for bringing us to this point and for giving us the commandments, we also petition for the rebuilding of the Temple and ultimate redemption.

IV. The Remainder of the Seder: Celebratory Observance in Freedom and Yearning for the Messianic Redemption

At this point, we observe the laws of Passover. Though there is no Passover offering, we eat the Matzah and Maror and then the festive meal (*shulhan 'orekh*). Our eating of the *korekh* (Hillel sandwich of Matzah, Maror, and Haroset together) reenacts a Temple observance (*Pesahim* 115a). Similarly, we pretend that the final piece of Matzah (*tzafun*) is the Passover offering, the last taste we should have in our

---

[9] Rabbi Joseph B. Soloveitchik, *Festival of Freedom: Essays on Passover and the Haggadah*, Joel B. Wolowelsky & Reuven Ziegler (eds.) (New York: The Toras Horav Foundation, by Ktav, 2006), p. 105.

mouths (*Pesahim* 119b).[10] By consuming the second half of the Matzah from *yahatz*, we take from the slavery Matzah and transform its other half into a symbol of freedom.

After the Grace after Meals (*barekh*), we pray for salvation from our enemies and ultimately for the messianic era. By reading the verses "pour out Your wrath" (*shefokh hamatekha*, Psa. 79:6-7), we express the truism that we cannot fully praise God in *hallel* until we sigh from enemy oppression and recognize contemporary suffering.[11] Many communities customarily open the door at this point for Elijah the Prophet, also expressing hope for redemption. We then recite the remainder of the *hallel*, which focuses on our redemption, as discussed above. Some of the later songs added to *nirtzah* likewise express these themes of festive singing and redemption.

V. Conclusion

The Haggadah is a composite text that expanded and evolved over the centuries. The symbols along with traditional explanations for their meanings likewise developed over time. In its current form, our Haggadah—with its core some 1000 years old—takes us on a remarkable journey that combines narrative and observance into an intellectual and experiential event for people of all ages and backgrounds. In this manner, we travel alongside

---

[10] The word *afikoman* derives from the Greek, referring to anything done at the end of a meal, such as eating dessert or playing music or revelry. This was a common after-dinner feature at Greco-Roman meals (cf. J.T. *Pesahim* 37d). The Sages of the Talmud understood that people needed to retain the taste of the Passover offering in their mouths. It was only in the 13th century that the Matzah we eat at the end of the meal was called the *afikoman* (Joseph Tabory, *JPS Commentary on the Haggadah*, p. 15).

[11] Shemuel & Ze'ev Safrai enumerate longer lists of related verses that some medieval communities added (*Haggadat Hazal*, pp. 174-175).

our ancestors from freedom to slavery to redemption. We are left with a conscious recognition that though we are free and we bless God for that; we long for the Temple in Jerusalem. *La-shanah ha-ba'ah be-Yerushalayim, Amen.*

To Be a Matzah[1]

Rabbi Nathan Lopes Cardozo

Instead of providing us with a straight answer, the Talmud responds by asking still another question. Why do people sin altogether? Understanding that people will continue to transgress, the Talmud tries to analyze the paradoxical situation in which many people find themselves: Man's desire to do well, and his constant encounter with his/her evil inclination. Realizing that this inclination is difficult to overcome, it suggests that human beings, especially Jews, should make the following declaration whenever they try to obey the laws of the Torah but fail to do so (*b. Berakhot* 17a):

> Lord of the Universe
> It is well known to You that it is our desire to do Your will
> But what prevents us?
> The yeast in the dough.

The expression "The yeast in the dough" is well known in the Talmud. It is the description for the evil impulse in human beings. The last is the one which is responsible for "all ferment in the human heart" and why man does not always behave the way he should.

We now understand the circuitous answer the Talmud provides to the original question concerning the reasons why it is forbidden to possess or consume leaven on Pesach. Leaven is after all used to cause the yeast in the dough to rise and in a literal sense it is exactly that which also causes bread to become bread which is forbidden on Pesach. In other words: It is the most distinct symbol of the cause of all human transgressions!

---

[1] This essay was written in 2008 and is part of a previous year's lengthy lecture on Pesah.

This, however, begs the question. Why is the evil inclination symbolized by leaven? What does leaven do wrong that it should be used as the symbol for the evil urge in man?

A closer look however reveals a most fascinating idea. Bread, chametz, is blown up matza. It is matza which went overboard and got wild. What after all, is the essential difference between both? They are made from exactly the same ingredients. It is only the speed which makes the difference between the two. If the dough is baked quickly you get matza. However, if the dough is left for a while, it will rise and after being baked turns into bread.

The only real difference between the two is therefore hot air. An ingredient of no real substance! And it is this substance which makes bread look powerful in comparison to matza. It rises, becoming haughty, giving the impression that it consists of a great amount of substance and abundance while in reality it mainly consists of hot air. The matza however is humble; there is no attempt to make more of itself than what it really contains: plain dough.

Bread, then, is an arrogant matza. And it is for this reason that it symbolizes the evil inclination since it is the attitude of haughtiness, blowing oneself up beyond one's real self which leads to undesirable acts which causes man to go astray. It is the source of all transgressions. Would a human being be humble, he or she would not contemplate doing anything wrong. Only arrogance leads man to undesirable deeds.

On Pesach, which symbolizes the beginning of the Jewish people, Jews are once more reminded that their mission to become a light unto the nations can only start in the spirit of humility. Arrogance can never be the foundation of spirituality and moral integrity. It cannot inspire others, nor will it have a lasting effect.

Consequently, the art achieving real life is to be like a matza in a world of chametz.[2] This is the reason, as understood by the Talmud, why one is prohibited to possess or eat chametz on Pesach. Only the matza is food of moral quality. May God allow us to serve Him in this spirit and grant us and the world the final redemption.

---

[2] Question to ponder on the Seder night table: Based on the above, why is chametz not prohibited throughout the whole year? For a possible answer, see bYoma 69b concerning the reluctance of the sages to imprison the *yetzer hara'*.

Three Aspects of the Korban Pesah

Rabbi Yitzchak Etshalom

As I proposed in the first volume of *Between The Lines of the Bible*,[1] we have – from one perspective – a distinct advantage over the original recipients of the Torah. Whereas they only had the knowledge of the particular piece of divine teaching that they were receiving and everything which came before, we have the information of the ages. Over three thousand years have passed since the events of that fateful evening in Egypt, and much information has been revealed and inferred about those events and their impact on Jewish history in the intervening years. Not only do we have the entire Torah as a reference point for understanding any piece of text – we also have millenia of interpretation and commentary.

This advantage can sometimes turn against us. In our attempt to understand the straightforward meaning (*p'shat*) of the text, our "larger picture" sometimes makes it difficult to see and hear the verses through the eyes and ears of the original target audience. In this essay, we will study a well-known passage, at the heart of the Exodus narrative, and note how differently it may have been understood by the "players" at the time.

I. Shemot 12:1-13:16 – A Confusing Text

The narrative which evolves from the plague cycle to the moment of liberation includes a description of the first stage of the Exodus of B'nei Yisrael from Egypt. A central feature in that stage is the *Korban Pesah* and its various attendant *Mitzvot*. These laws are presented throughout Chapter 12 (and, in a tangential manner, in the first 16 verses of Chapter 13) of Shemot. The narrative of the

---

[1] Yashar Books, 2006.

smiting of the firstborn and the first steps of actual departure are intertwined with these laws, along with two separate "concluding" statements announcing the climactic end to our slavery.

This entire section (12:1-13:16) seems to lack unity and flow. I hope to provide an explanation of the basic components in this section of text which will not only "restore" the unity, but will also shed some light on the central feature in the Passover celebration – the *Korban Pesah.*

II. Outline and Questions

It will be helpful to preface our discussion by outlining the various segments of the text in question:

12:1-20 – "*Parashat haHodesh*" (God speaks to Moses and Aaron)
The New Moon, some *Mitzvot* of the *Korban Pesah* and the *Mitzvot* regarding eating Matzah, bitter herbs and avoiding & destroying Hametz and leavening agents ("*S'or*").

12:21-28 (Moses speaks to the elders of the nation)
Moses' charge to the elders regarding some details of the offering and how to respond to future generations who ask about it.

12:29-36 (narrative)
The plague of the first-born, Pharaoh's midnight call to Moses to take B'nei Yisra'el out; B'nei Yisra'el "borrow" the gold, silver and clothing of the Egyptians.

12:37-42 (narrative)
Israelites travel from Ra'mses to Sukkot, including the statement, "At the end of the 430 years, to the very day, all Hashem's divisions left Egypt" (v. 41).

12:43-50 (God speaks to Moses and Aaron)
More *Mitzvot* of the *Korban Pesah*, including who may partake of it.

12:51 (narrative)
"And on that very day Hashem brought the Israelites out of Egypt by their divisions" (v. 51).

13:1-2 (God speaks to Moses)
The *Mitzvah* regarding the sanctification of the firstborn.

13:3-16 (Moses speaks to B'nei Yisra'el)
The *Mitzvot* of remembering the Exodus, avoiding consumption of *Hametz*, not owning *Hametz*, teaching children about the event, T'fillin, sanctification of the firstborn and, again(!?) T'fillin.

As can be easily seen from this all-too-brief outline, there are a number of anomalies – both in sequence and in substance – in this text:

1. Why are the details of the *Korban Pesah* given in two different sections (12:1-20 and 43-50)?
2. Why does Moses present a series of *Mitzvot* (Hametz; telling the children about the Exodus; T'fillin) before informing B'nei Yisra'el about the sanctification of the firstborn— when that was the only command the God gave him at that time (13:2)?
3. Why is the Mitzvah of T'fillin given twice (13:9, 16)?
4. Why is the Exodus declared twice (12:41, 51)?

III. Looking Through the Eyes of B'nei Yisra'el in Egypt

As I noted in the introduction to this essay, we need to step back from what we know and assume the role of the original audience to capture the full impact of the text.

In our case, we have to look at each section of text and pay close attention to what was known – and what was not yet known – to Moses, Pharaoh and to B'nei Yisra'el.

Although Moses (and Pharaoh) knew about the impending *Makkat B'khorot* (smiting of the firstborn; see Exodus 11:1-5; see also 4:22-23), it is unclear as to whether the Israelites knew about it at all. In addition, no one (up until this point) knew what night the plague would take place (see Nahmanides 11:4).

Besides this background of lack-of-information (against which the text in Chapter 12 must be seen), a simple reading of the text indicates that B'nei Yisra'el had little knowledge of the laws and practices regarding animal offerings. Therefore, to comprehend the perspective of the Israelites at the time, and whatever symbolism is being conveyed through these commandments, we must look at the verses through these "new eyes" – the eyes of the Israelites in Egypt at that time.

IV. Aspect #1: The Korban "In Lieu" – A Celebration of Salvation

In his explanation of the meaning behind animal offerings, Nahmanides (commentary to Leviticus 1:9) suggests that the person bringing the offering should view himself as if he were on the altar. The catharsis of a Korban is achieved when the owner experiences his own sacrifice vicariously through the offering.

Although, as pointed out above, this was not something that the Israelites would know from the yet-unrevealed *Hilkhot Ma'aseh haKorbanot* (the Laws of Offerings) – they would know it from their own history. The first and earliest Korban in national memory was the ram that was brought by Abraham on Mount Moriah in lieu of his son, Yitzhak (Genesis 22:13). This occurred when Yitzhak, who was (in a manner) supposed to be offered up to God, was spared.

It is reasonable to assume that when the Israelites were commanded to offer up a lamb or goat on the afternoon of the fourteenth day of the first month, they made the obvious and immediate association with Isaac's ram and understood this upcoming Korban to be some sort of a "substitution" offering. When they were informed (12:12) about the imminent slaying of the firstborn throughout Egypt (note– not just "Egyptians" but *throughout the land of Egypt*"), they understood that this upcoming offering was to stand in place of their own firstborn children, who stood in mortal danger of dying on that night. This explains why the Torah specifically commands each family to take one animal for sacrifice (12:3 – representing the *b'khor* [firstborn] of that household) and why the blood of the offering was to be daubed on the doorposts and top-jamb of each house – as if to "mark" the house, indicating that the *b'khor* of this family (=his animal substitute) has already been slaughtered.

(We might entertain a more radical understanding of the identity of the Israelite target group: In 4:22, the Israelites are identified as God's "*b'khor*"; that being the case, every member of the Israelites was under threat of death with the upcoming *Makkat B'khorot*, and the animal and its blood stood as a representative for that person and his household. This would explain the odd phrasing: "...the entire congregation of Israel shall slaughter it..." [12:6]. The use of a member of the flock [v. 5] is particularly powerful in its symbolic association; not only is their leader, Moses, a shepherd by profession (3:1), but he himself compares the Israelites to a flock in need of a shepherd after his death

[Bemidbar 27:17]. Either approach to understanding the endangered people for whom the offering "stands in"– the actual firstborn or the entire B'nei Yisra'el – is consistent with the approach outlined below.)

V. Aspect #2: The Korban of Fire: A Celebration of the End of Slavery

There are additional laws of the *Korban Pesah* as detailed in *Parashat HaHodesh* (12:8-11) which reflect a different aspect of the Korban. Whereas the first group of commands (taking the animal into the house, slaughtering on the afternoon of the fourteenth, daubing the blood etc.) reflect the "substitution" or "redemptive" aspect of the Korban (as explained above), the next group seem to have one thing in common– they represent and celebrate the end of the slavery experience. Let's look at the details:

a) The Korban must be roasted (v. 8) – symbolic of the "fiery furnace" of Egypt which was our oppressed life there (see Deuteronomy 4:20, I Kings 8:51, Jeremiah 11:4).

b) The Korban must be eaten with matzot and maror (bitter herbs, v. 8) – both symbols of oppression and poverty. Eating these is symbolic of mastery over the experience.

c) The Korban must be eaten entire and not broken up (v. 9) – symbolizing that the Israelites (represented by the animal as explained above) have come through the experience complete.

d) None of the Korban's meat may be left over (v. 10) – symbolizing that the entire experience is to be completed tonight and that every member of the nation will be redeemed and taken out of the oppression. (Also, any leftover meat must be burned– again the theme of fire.)

e) The people are to eat the Korban "sitting on their suitcases," implying that the experience is complete and that their station is about to change.

Subsequent to the presentation of these specific Halakhot, God tells Moses the reason behind them: "I will pass through Egypt on this night...and the blood will be an *ot* (sign) for you on the houses..." (vv. 12-13). After this, God instructs Moses that there should be an eternal commemoration of this day – "And this day will be for you a *zikkaron* (commemoration), celebrating it as a festival for Hashem..." (v. 14).

The last 6 verses of *Parashat HaHodesh* outline the basic Halakhot of eating Matzah, destroying Hametz, avoiding the eating of Hametz, the "holiday" nature of the first and seven days of this future festival, and the reason for this festival (which does not at all include the *Korban Pesah*): "...for on this very day I (will) have taken all of your divisions out of the land of Egypt..." (v. 17). We are then given additional dimensions of the prohibitions of Hametz.

Summary of *Parashat HaHodesh* (12:1-20)

Note that the *Korban Pesah* in no way is associated with the imminent Exodus. It inheres two celebrations only – the salvation from the plague of the firstborn and end of slavery. This day will be the first of an annual seven day festival, celebrating the Exodus – but that festival, at this point, only includes the Hametz/Matzah component and does not include the *Korban Pesah*.

VI. Moses' Instructions to the Elders (12:21-28)

In the next Parashah (12:21-28), Moses relates part of God's command to the elders of the Israelites (and, from the context, this information is passed on to all of the people; see vv. 27-28). Note that he only tells them about the *Korban Pesah* (with the addition of the bunch of *ezov* [hyssop]; more on that below) and that that celebration should be perpetuated for generations. He only instructs them that this will be a celebration of salvation, as we can see from the response he commands we give to our children when they ask us as to the meaning of this offering: "You shall declare, it is a Pesah offering to God, Who passed over the houses of the Israelites when he attacked Egypt and saved our houses..." (v. 27)

In other words, the only perspective that Moses gave to the people before the actual event took place was the salvation. He did not inform them that they were leaving– just that, at some future time, they would be in the Land of Canaan and would have to explain this celebration to their children.

As noted above, there is one additional aspect to the *Korban Pesah* presented in this instruction. "Take a bunch of *ezov* (some type of grass or herb – the medieval commentators debate its meaning, although the general consensus leads to hyssop) and dip it into the blood [of the offering] which is in the vessel, and daub it on the upper-door-jamb and the doorposts..." (v. 22). This is an additional symbol of the end of slavery (as above), that the Israelites – who were lowly like the grass of the field – would now be gathered together (remember that they must spend the whole night indoors with the whole family together) and elevated to God's worship– thus culminating their servitude to Pharaoh. Again, note that there is no mention of leaving Egypt– just being liberated from slavery.

VII. Narratives

Narrative #1: Makkat B'khorot (12:29-36)

As the text moves from instruction to narrative, we are told about the terrible fate of the first-borns throughout

Egypt (note v. 29– non-Egyptians also died!). Pharaoh comes to Moses and Aaron and "throws them out" of Egypt.

Narrative #2: First Steps Out of Egypt (12:37-42)

Now we are told that the Israelites marched from Ra'mses (their working town– see 1:11) to Sukkot– which is still in Egypt. At this point, we are given a sense of conclusion– how many years the Israelites were in Egypt and that exactly on that day, they left. Note that in v. 41, we are told that B'nei Yisra'el left Egypt– not that God took them out! In the next verse, we are told that the night (before) was a "guarded night" of God– but their actual first steps happened of their own accord. Pharaoh banished them and they left.

Let's summarize what information B'nei Yisra'el had as they finished the first leg of their march and arrived at Sukkot on the morning after the plague.

1) They have been told that the salvation (from being killed) which they just experienced must be commemorated, via the *Korban Pesah* in the future.

2) Their slavery is over and they have left their slave-town (Ra'mses) BUT

3) They haven't been told that they are going to the Land of Canaan (or, indeed, even leaving Egypt at all) NOR

4) Do they know about any special relationship which they are destined to have with God.

Keep in mind that the promise presented earlier (6:6-8) that God would take them out of the bonds of Egypt, save them from their work, redeem them with an outstretched arm and great wonders and would take them to be His nation– this entire promise was not "heard" by the Israelites (6:9) due to their overwhelming sense of servitude.

VIII. The Law of the Pesah (*Hukkat Happesah*; 12:43-50)

At this point, we are given a second set of details regarding the *Korban Pesah*, coming under the heading of *Hukkat haPesah* (the eternal statute of the *Korban Pesah*). Following our chronological sequencing of the text, these Halakhot were given to Moses and Aaron at Sukkot, the morning after the plague. These include the definition of who may partake of the Korban (only B'nei Yisra'el), that anyone joining the community must undergo B'rit Milah (the covenant of circumcision) and two laws which correspond to details we saw earlier:

a) The Korban must stay inside the house in which it is eaten;

b) No bone may be broken in the *Korban Pesah*.

What is the significance of these "new" details and why were they given in a separate Parashah from *Parashat HaHodesh*– and after the Israelites were part of the way out of Egypt?

Aspect #3: The Korban of Completion: A Celebration of Fulfillment of the Covenant "Between The Pieces" (*B'rit Bein Hab'tarim*)

Even a cursory glance at verses 43-50 brings an immediate association: The new demand that only a member of the covenant who has been circumcised may partake in the *Korban Pesah* reminds us of Abraham– the original member of that covenant (see Genesis 17). How would an Israelite in Egypt, knowing the family history and traditions, understand the inclusion of Abraham in his or her current narrative?

In Genesis 15, we are told about an earlier covenant which God made with Abram (not yet Abraham) regarding his descendants (vv. 13-14)[2] :

> ...Know for certain that your descendants will be strangers in a country not their own, and they will be enslaved and mistreated four hundred years. But I will punish the nation they serve as slaves, and afterward they will come out with great possessions.

This promise – which points directly to the enslavement and Exodus from Egypt – was confirmed through a ceremony in which Avram took animals (including a goat and a ram) and divided them in half. When darkness fell, Avram – who was already outside (see v. 5) – saw a fire pass between the halves, consummating the "Covenant Between the Pieces" (*B'rit bein haB'tarim*), as it is commonly called.

Now we understand the Abraham-Exodus connection– and can look back at the original presentation (12:1-20) and understand some of the details in a new light. The fire which appears in three consecutive verses (12:8-10) reminds us of the fire which consummated the *B'rit bein haB'tarim*. In addition, this is the only Korban which had to be completely devoured at night– which again reminds us of the *B'rit bein haB'tarim*. Once we have that association, we immediately notice the contrasts (the Torah often compares events in order to demonstrate their differences). Unlike the *B'rit*-promise, this one must take place indoors; and, unlike the *B'rit*-promise, the animal here must be complete. These Halakhot are re-presented in our section (*Hukkat haPesah*)– in verse 46. What has happened? The *B'rit bein haB'tarim* has now been fulfilled. The broken animal is now whole and the "outsiders" are now indoors.

---

[2] See volume 1, ch. 10.

Suddenly, our entire perspective on the process has changed. Instead of "merely" having been saved from a terrible plague and having the yoke of slavery lifted (which is all we know up until this point), we now understand that the ancient promise of God has finally been fulfilled. The celebration of the *Korban Pesah* takes on a whole new light. Instead of us leaving as a result of Pharaoh's order, we are now being taken out by God, with our destiny to be His people lying immediately ahead of us.

This explains the "second" exodus verse (v. 51). In this verse, instead of stating that B'nei Yisra'el left– it says that God took them out!

IX. The Sanctification of the First-Born *(Kiddush B'khorot)*

At the beginning of Chapter 13, God gives Moses one Mitzvah– to sanctify the human and animal first-born to Him. Earlier, we asked why Moses doesn't just give this Mitzvah and why he prefaces it with other Mitzvot (including some he was given earlier), such as Hametz & Matzah, teaching the children about the Exodus and T'fillin.

As mentioned above (end of section VI), there was a four-tiered promise which God related to Moses before the onset of the plague-driven negotiations with Pharaoh. God promised that He would:

1) Take us out (*v'hotzeiti*) of the bondage of Egypt;
2) Save us (*v'hitzalti*) from their work;
3) Redeem us (*v'ga'alti*) and
4) Take us to Him (*v'lakachti..li*) as a nation.

As we have already seen, three of these promises were already fulfilled (out of order):

#3: We were redeemed when we were not killed on the night of the smiting of the firstborn. (Parenthetically, the term *g'ulah* can also mean a redemption of substitution– see Ruth 4:7.)

#2: We were saved from their work when Pharaoh bade us leave his land.

#1: We were taken out when God turned our exit to Exodus with *Hukkat haPesah* (as above).

The one component that remains to be fulfilled is for B'nei Yisra'el to become God's nation. "*Kadesh LI* (sanctify to me) every b'khor...*LI hu* (they are Mine). The word *li*, meaning "they are mine", which is used twice here, evokes the fourth promise: *v'lakachti et'khem LI l'am*– (and I will take you unto Me as a nation). Kiddush haB'khorot is (at least the first stage of) the fulfillment of this promise.

The Israelites already know that they must celebrate the "redemption" of the night of the plague and the "being saved" from slavery. Moses has to communicate the rest of the process to the people– that they must celebrate and commemorate being taken out of Egypt and becoming God's nation.

First, Moses presents them with the commemoration of being taken out:

1: Remember the day of the Exodus (13:3)

2: Hametz and Matzah (13:6-7) (laws which remind us of the actual departure– remember, this had not been communicated yet).

3: Teaching the children about the Exodus (v. 8)– note that this time, the information to be given by the parent to the child is not about the plague of the first-born, rather it is about the Exodus.

4: T'fillin (v. 9)– a constant reminder of the Exodus. The hand T'fillin are to be an *ot l'kha*– a "sign for you", indicating a sign for you to see and which will remind us– and the head T'fillin are to be a *zikkaron*– again a commemoration for you to remember that God took us out. This wording is nearly identical to the two terms used to describe the blood on the doors (*ot lakhem*) and the celebration of that day (*zikkaron*).

5: Kiddush B'khorot (vv. 10-13). Now that the celebration of *v'hotzeiti* is complete, Moses informs them about Kiddush B'khorot– the fulfillment of the fourth step– *v'lakachti*.

6: Informing the children (vv. 14-15). The son's question is not about the Exodus or about the *Korban Pesah* (or about Hametz & Matzah)– it is about *Kiddush B'khorot*.

7: T'fillin (v. 16). Note what has changed– the *ot l'kha* (a sign for you) has become an *ot* (sign)– indicating that it is now (also) a sign for others. The *zikkaron* is now *totafot*– which is a type of jewelry not unlike a crown.[3]

The T'fillin, first presented as a commemorative device by which we remind ourselves of *v'hotzeiti*– now become a sign for the rest of the world and a crown– as we are now God's nation with the fulfillment of *v'lakachti* through the vehicle of Kiddush B'khorot.

X. Afterword

Although our three thousand (plus) years of accumulated tradition, interpretation and hindsight give us a broad understanding of the meaning of the *Korban Pesah* (and, indeed, all of the composite sections of the Exodus narrative), we can often gain greater insight, counter-intuitively, by "erasing" what we know and assuming the "awareness base" of the original audience and – to the extent possible – walking through their evolving understanding of the impact of events and commands as history unfolds before their eyes.

---

[3] See Mishnah Shabbat 6:1, Radak's Michlol, "Haskel v'Yadoaʻ."

Massah U'Maror

Rabbi Raymond Harari

The most prominent items at the Passover *seder* are the *massah* and *maror*. Indeed, Rabban Gamliel teaches us that the Passover *seder* would be incomplete without the presence of both these food items:

רבן גמליאל היה אומר: כל-מי שלא אמר שלשה דברים אלו בפסח לא יצא ידי חובתו: פסח, *מצה, ומרור.*

> Rabban Gamliel said: Whoever does not make mention of [i.e. explain] these three things on passover does not discharge his duty, and these are they: The passover-offering; *Unleavened bread; and bitter herbs.*

Not surprisingly, they bring to the table dramatically different motifs. The *massah* represents the exodus from Egypt while the *maror* represents the slavery itself. The *massah*, bread in its unleavened state, expresses G-d's impatience in delivering us from the hands of the Egyptians. For all future generations we would know that G-d's rush in taking us out of Egypt would be symbolized by bread that was not allowed to rise. The *maror*, on the other hand, reminds us of the bitterness of our oppression and the evils of the demonic power that ruled over the people of Israel for centuries.

These two food items, therefore, capture the essence of the holiday of Passover. They remind us of our obligation to connect to our forefathers and our history in the fullest sense: the good and the ugly, the exhilarating and the depressing. Much like the holiday of Purim that we celebrated a month ago, Passover reminds us of the unusual turns that our lives as the Jewish people have taken. We

47

have witnessed the worst of what humankind has dealt others and the best of what G-d has rewarded His people. In our own times, our people were both slaughtered during the Holocaust years and witnessed the miraculous rebirth of the Jewish people in its homeland.

Passover reminds us that both experiences and emotions are part of what it means to be a Jew. And by connecting to the messages that the *massah* and the *maror* send us, we propel ourselves to strengthen our relationship to the Almighty.

Arami Oved Avi – Peshat and Derash

Rabbi Alex Israel

We all begin the Seder with intense anticipation and feelings of excitement. We make Kiddush, drink the first cup, *Karpas*, *Afikoman* hunting ensues, then *Mah Nishtana* from our ever so sweet nephew, and then we begin *Maggid*, listening to Divrei Torah, asking, discussing. It's great! But by the time we reach "*Tzei Ulemad*," we've had Devar Torah overload – we're thinking about the meal…"How many pages to *Dayyenu*?"

Well, my task here is to enlighten one corner of the Haggada that is pretty strange for any of you adherents of *peshat*, and hopefully to encourage just a little more attention to this fascinating passage of the Seder.

I. Chavruta Study

1. Look at the *parasha* of "*Arami Oved Avi*" in *Devarim* 26:1-10. What is the farmer trying to express with the statements that he pronounces at the Mikdash?
2. *Arami Oved Avi*: See Rashi, Rashbam, Ibn Ezra.
3. Why does the Haggada read this phrase differently?

II. The Origins of the Seder

The origins of the Seder may be found in the Mishna. The closing chapter of *Massekhet Pesachim*[1] outlines the bare bones of the Seder that we know and love. There we read:

---

[1] See http://www.vbm-torah.org/pesach/pes63-aw.htm for a literary analysis of the chapter (by Rabbi Avraham Walfish).

They pour out the second cup.

It is now that the son asks, 'Why is this night different...'[2]

And the father teaches the son according to the son's intelligence and aptitude.

He begins with the negative and ends with the positive, and engages in a *derash* of *Arami Oved Avi* until the entire *parasha* is complete.

So here we have the skeleton of our *Maggid*. It begins with questions. The father then responds. The story is to be told beginning with the negative[3] – the slavery and harsh beginning of Jewish History – and to end with the positive – the freedom, the sense of Godliness that *Am Yisrael* discover as their identity. This night tells an optimistic narrative – from bad to good – "and they all lived happily ever after."

But then, we have a few enigmatic words from the Mishna: "And he [the father – the teacher] engages in a *derash* of *Arami Oved Avi* until the entire *parasha* is complete." What is *Arami Oved Avi*? Why does it have a place in our Seder? Why are we asked to use the medium of "*derash*?" Let us understand what is happening here.

III. The Basics

Arami Oved Avi is probably the most concise description in the Torah of the enslavement-Exodus

---

[2] At this point the entire *Ma Nishtana* is written out, with differences appropriate to Temple times.

[3] The Talmud disputes the precise identity of this "negative to positive" narrative. One view sees the story to be told as one of national freedom from oppression. The other opinion wants to tell a more religious story of the transition from pre-Abrahamic paganism to the monotheistic beliefs of the Israelite nation. In practice our Haggada incorporates both opinions.

drama.[4] It may be found in Devarim 26:5-10 (and if you are unfamiliar with it, I strongly recommend glancing at the entire chapter there to gain some context.) The *parasha* of *Arami Oved Avi* is taken from the "First Fruits" ceremony in which an Israelite farmer would present the first fruits (of the 7 species of Eretz Yisrael) to the Temple. This presentation was accompanied by a formal verbal declaration. The declaration took the following form:

> "A wandering Aramean was my father. He went down to Egypt with meager numbers and sojourned there; but there he became a great and very populous nation. The Egyptians dealt harshly with us and oppressed us; they imposed heavy labor upon us. We cried to the LORD, the God of our fathers, and the LORD heard our plea and saw our plight, our misery, and our oppression. The LORD freed us from Egypt by a mighty hand, by an outstretched arm and awesome power, and by signs and portents. He brought us to this place and gave us this land, a land flowing with milk and honey. Wherefore I now bring the first fruits of the soil which You, O LORD, have given me." (Devarim 26: 5-10)

Let us begin by examining the methodology that *Chazal* employed in their reading of this passage on *Leil HaSeder*. What *Chazal* actually did is take each phrase and try to discover some deeper meaning, either an assumption or an intention, or even a hint or a Biblical paralleled phrase that might shed some light upon the story at hand, the story of the Exodus. This process of digging under and between and around the words is the process we know as "*derash*" or *Midrash* – a Rabbinic methodology that aims to uncover and discover allusions, subtexts, implications and assumptions in any and every passage of the Bible.

---

[4] For an excellent presentation as to why we choose this particular parasha to tell the story of the Exodus, see Rabbi Shaviv's article - http://www.vbm-torah.org/pesach/ys-hag.htm on the VBM.

What does the Haggada do with this passage? Here is a sample:

> **"And he went down to Egypt"** forced by Divine decree. "And he sojourned there" - this teaches that our father Jacob did not go down to Egypt to settle, but only to live there temporarily. Thus it is said, "They said to Pharaoh, We have come to sojourn in the land, for there is no pasture for your servants' flocks because the hunger is severe in the land of Canaan; and now, please, let your servants dwell in the land of Goshen."
>
> **"Few in number"** as it is said: "Your fathers went down to Egypt with seventy persons, and now, the Lord, your G-d, has made you as numerous as the stars of heaven."
>
> **"And he became there a nation"** this teaches that Israel was distinctive there.
>
> **"Great, mighty,"** as it is said: "And the children of Israel were fruitful and increased abundantly, and multiplied and became very, very mighty, and the land became filled with them."

The opening phrases for each paragraph come from verse 5. The Haggada takes each phrase of verse 5, and scrutinizes it, commenting upon its hidden assumptions. This is the process of *derash*. By this method, we emphasize that our tenure in Egypt was supposed to be temporary even though it became permanent, that Israelites were "distinct" in Egypt, and many other fascinating points.

IV. The Peshat of *Arami Oved Avi*

What I would like to comment upon however is the manner in which the author of the *derash* masterfully manipulates this Torah passage and harnesses it to the aim at hand, namely, the Exodus story. Let me elaborate and explain.

The *parasha* in Devarim 26 describes a farmer bringing his first fruits to the Mikdash. There, he recites "*Arami Oved Avi*". What is the thrust, the purpose, the message of this declaration?

The entire declaration revolves around the issues of homelessness and homecoming. Let us explain. The farmer arrives with his basket of fruits at the Temple. He presents his fruits to the Kohen and then makes a rather bizarre statement:

> "I declare this day before the Lord God that I have come to the land that the Lord swore to our fathers to assign to us." (26:3)

Who is this man? He is a farmer who might have been born and raised in *Eretz Yisrael*. He might have never left the country all his life. His family has owned the tribal inheritance for centuries, and yet, he stands at the Mikdash and declares: "I have come to the land!" What sort of a statement is this?

I think that the next paragraph *Arami Oved Avi* enlightens us. It begins with the story of "A wandering Aramean," that our ancestors were homeless. And it takes us through the fate of how their lack of home lead them to Egypt, where indeed the nation expanded greatly, but was enslaved harshly. The people cry to God, God saves them, and then:

> He brought us to this place, and has given us this land, a land flowing with milk and honey. And now, behold, I have brought the first of the fruit of the land, which You, O Hashem, have given me.

In other words, "Thank You God for giving me a land that I can call my own, that I can farm, that I can build. We were homeless for so long, and oppressed, but now we have a place to call our own, all because of You Hashem."

V. Who is the "Wandering Aramean"?

We are all familiar with the explanation of this phrase in the Haggada. The Haggada translates it as "An Aramean–Lavan – (sought to) destroy my father (Yaakov.)" Is this the correct reading? After all, we have translated it thus far as "My father was a wandering Aramean."

And which of our "fathers" might have been a wandering Aramean?

> "Our father Abraham originated from Aram.[5] He wandered in a state of exile from Aram, as it states: 'Go forth from your land'[6]" (Rashbam).

> "Were the 'Aramean' referring to Lavan, the Hebrew would have to read "*ma'avid*" or "*me'abed*" (and not '*oved*). Moreover (in the context of the *parasha* in Devarim) what logic would there be in the statement, 'Lavan wanted to kill my father, and he went down to Egypt?' Lavan had no hand in causing Yaakov to descend to Egypt! Rather, we should suggest that the Aramean is Yaakov, and the verses meaning is this. That when Yaakov was in Aram, he was an "*oved*" i.e. poor, penniless – proofs from Mishlei 31:6,7 – and the point here is that I did not inherit the land from my father (Yaakov) for he was poverty stricken when he came to Aram. He was even a stranger in Egypt ..." (Ibn Ezra)

Both the Rashbam and the Ibn Ezra weave this phrase very naturally into the *parasha* in Devarim, both grammatically and thematically. Again, the theme of the

---

[5] See Bereshit 12:4-5 Avraham sets out from Haran to Canaan. Later in 27:43 and 28:2 Haran and (Padan-) Aram are synonyms for the region in which Lavan resided. So it would appear that Aram and Haran are the same place. Similarly, in 24:20, Rivka is described as originating from Aram Naharayim.

[6] Bereshit 12:1.

parasha is homelessness and homecoming. The Rashbam says that the Aramean is Avraham, who wandered from his birthplace Aram. In that case, *Arami Oved Avi* transcribes Jewish History from the moment that Abraham leaves his original home[7] and is promised the Land of Israel, until the moment in which the promise is fulfilled, and his progeny settle therein.

The Ibn Ezra makes two points. First, he proves the grammatical impossibility of the Haggada's reading. He then suggests that the Aramean is Yaakov, who dwelt with Lavan in Aram. The intention once again, is to stress how our forefathers had no land, and therefore, the Land of Israel is a gift only by virtue of God to *Am Yisrael*.

But our basic thesis is reinforced. The *parasha* in Devarim is about being a wanderer and then achieving a permanent home. That is the central message. God is praised and thanked for his role in granting the Jewish People a permanent abode.

VI. The Derash of *"Arami Oved Avi"*

However, the Haggada reads it differently. And I would like to spend some time thinking about what the *Ba'al*

---

[7] Some might find it strange that Avraham rather than Yaakov be the Aramean. After all, it was Yaakov who initiated the Egyptian exile, taking the family down during the years of famine. Indeed the opening lines of Shemot testify to this.

Two points are worth making here: First, the notion of beginning the Exodus story with Avraham (rather than Yaakov who actually went down to Egyopt thereby starting the Galut) is clear in many places in Tanach. See Joshua 24:2, pesukim quoted in the Haggada, which begins the Exodus story with Avaraham. Likewise Nechemia 9:7-15.

Second, since Devarim 26 is focused upon Eretz Yisrael, we should note that it is to Avraham that the promises of Eretz Yisrael are made at every stage. See Bereshit 12:7; 13:14-18; 15:7, 18; 17:7-8. See also 26:3. The centrality of Avraham in God's promises of the Land cannot be over stressed. Hence Avraham's appearance in a parasha that spotlights the theme of Eretz Yisrael is more than natural.

Hahaggada was thinking about when he reworked this passage. Here is the Hagadda's version:

> Go forth and learn what Laban the Aramean wanted to do to our father Jacob. Pharaoh had issued a decree against the male children only, but Laban wanted to uproot everything - as it is said: "The Aramean wished to destroy my father; and he went down to Egypt and sojourned there, few in number; and he became there a nation - great and mighty and numerous."

Now it is true that in the Torah, Lavan is the only person to be described as "HaArami."[8] Lavan is THE Biblical Aramean—with a capital 'A.' And yet, let us ask ourselves, did Lavan ever seek to "uproot everything?" Even if we can deflect the grammatical discomfort of the Ibn Ezra, where do we read that Lavan wanted to destroy Yaakov in some way? Yes, he switched his wages, his daughters and wasn't particularly nice to Yaakov. But was he that bad? How do we justify the Hagadda's Midrashic reading?

We shall make an attempt to support this Midrash and our thesis shall be simple. Lavan didn't want to destroy Yaakov by killing him. Rather, he sought to keep Yaakov in Aram. Why? He didn't want his daughters or his grandchildren to leave. He wanted to make more money out of Yaakov, the master-shepherd. Maybe there are other factors here, but the bottom line is that Lavan tried to prevent Yaakov's departure. And what effect would that have had? Had Yaakov raised his family in Lavan's home, very soon they would have become subsumed within the wider "House of Lavan" and in time, would have entirely lost their identity as "the House of Abraham." The legacy of Avraham would have been lost forever, and the result would have been that there would have been no Jewish Nation. Let us substantiate these claims.

---

[8] Bereshit 25:10; 28:5; 31:20,24.

VII. Leaving Lavan

> "After Rachel had borne Joseph, Yaakov said to Lavan, 'Give me my wives and my children, for whom I served you, that I may go...'" (30:25-26)

Yaakov has a family. Even Rachel, his favorite wife, has borne a child. He has twelve children. It is time to go home.

But, Lavan persuades him to stay. He offers him a higher salary, a chance to get rich and Yaakov agrees. He remains there for quite a while, another six years, and at the end of this period he has amassed a large herd:

> Lavan's sons were saying, 'Jacob has taken all that was our father's and from that which was our father's he has built up all this wealth.' Jacob also saw that Lavan's manner towards him was not as it had been in the past. Then the Lord said to Jacob, 'Return to the land of your fathers where you were born and I will be with you.' (31:1-2)

Yaakov consults with his wives, who encourage him that now is the time to leave. And without hesitation, the family mount camels and leave with all their livestock, to return to Canaan.

> On the third day[9], Lavan was told that Yaakov had fled. So he took his kinsmen with him and pursued him a distance of seven days, catching up with him in the hill country of Gilead. God appeared to Lavan the Aramean in a dream by night and said to him, 'Beware of attempting anything with Yaakov[10], good or

---

[9] The parallel to *Yetziat Mitzrayim* is amplified by the Midrash. See Rashi to Shemot 14:4 where he suggests that Pharaoh was informed on the 3rd day of Israel's escape, and on the 7th day they catch up with them. See more in note 11.

[10] This phrase and also 31:29 that give us an impression that Lavan was planning or considering something a little more insidious than a peace

bad.'…Lavan caught up with Yaakov ….And said, 'What did you mean by sneaking off, and carrying off *my* daughters like prisoners of war…you didn't let me kiss *my* sons and *my* daughters…' (31:22-28)

What follows in an exceptionally strained discussion between Yaakov and Lavan in which accusations are made by Lavan and Yaakov. At the end of the conversation, Yaakov protests his integrity and honesty:

> These twenty years have I been in thy house: I served thee fourteen years for your two daughters, and six years for thy flock; and you have changed my wages ten times. Were it not that the God of my father, the God of Abraham, and the Fear of Isaac, had been on my side, surely now you would have sent me away empty handed…And Laban answered and said to Jacob: 'The daughters are my daughters, and the children are my children, and the flocks are my flocks, and all that you see is mine.' (31:41-43)

The entire narrative revolves around a single argument. To whom do the women, children and livestock belong: Yaakov or Lavan?[11]

Lavan sees everything as his: Yaakov has no right to leave. He has no rights to his children. They are Lavan's

---

covenant. This might be a further source, or support for the view that suggests that Lavan's true intentions were to kill Yaakov.

[11] There would appear to be many connection points between the stories of Lavan and the Exodus. Both are stories of "escape" from enslavement of sort. Both are headed to *Eretz Yisrael*. Both involve the "survival" of the minority group who are under threat by the host majority group. In addition, many phrases in Bereshit 31 are echoed in *Yetziat Mitzrayim*. The roots BaRaCH, RaDaPH, he chase, God's night-time intervention and the meeting in the morning. This point brings me to one of the more fascinating parallels between the. Two stories. Both here and in Shemot, there is a struggle over the children and even the animals! See Shemot 10:9-11: "We will all go, young and old: we must go with our sons and daughters, our flocks and herds…"

sons and Lavan's daughters.[12] Lavan wants Yaakov to stay. By leaving, Yaakov is stealing and betraying Lavan. Lavan expects Yaakov to remain forever in Aram.

But does Yaakov have no right to carve out his own future, to develop his own independent identity? We all know the implications of Lavan's plan, of Yaakov remaining in Aram. If they stay in Aram, they will most definitely be subsumed into the greater "House of Lavan." Yaakov's children will indeed be Lavan's children. That will be their primary identity. They will not be the children of Avraham, Yitzchak and Yaakov. They will grow up in Aram, develop Aramean accents, Aramean mores, and the command of "Lech Lecha" will be reversed. If Yaakov remains in Aram, there will be no *Bnei Yisrael* (literally, children of Israel i.e. Yaakov.) We are talking about the end of Jewish History before it has even begun!

Of course, God did not let that happen. Yaakov did not let that happen. But it might have happened. "Lavan sought to uproot everything?" Yes, everything! If Lavan had succeeded, then *Am Yisrael* would never have come into existence.

VIII. Back to the Haggadah

The Haggadah does much more than rework the phrase "*Arami Oved Avi.*" It also curtails the *parasha* and entirely omits the last two verses of the *Bikkurim* statement. It erases the lines that deal with *Eretz Yisrael*. This is with good reason. The Haggada manipulates Devarim 26 with tremendous skill, in order to harness it for the purpose of *Seder* Night – the retelling of the story of *Yetziat Mitzrayim*.

---

[12] Even at the very end of the story, after Lavan has agreed to separate from Yaakov, Lavan still insists that these are HIS daughters and HIS children. See 31:55.

Thus far, we have suggested that the declaration of Devarim 26 is about "Homelessness and Homecoming." But that is not the story of *Seder* Night. *Seder* night is about survival, freedom, God's might, the reversal of fortunes and the end of persecution.

The Haggada reworks Devarim 26 in a number of ways. First, it simply curtails the *parasha*, ending not with the entry into the Land, but rather with God's mighty hand of salvation. So this is a story of divine redemption.

But if the theme is "Persecution and Redemption," then the *peshat* of the opening phrase – *Arami Oved Avi* – that deals with homelessness is also sorely out of place! The Midrash re-reads, or reinterprets this phrase. In the eyes of the Midrash, it is not about a homeless ancestor; rather, it is about the dangers that have befallen the Jewish nation from Time immemorial. This is a story of the survival of the Jews, of persecution and salvation.

Into this framework, *Arami Oved Avi* fits perfectly in its Midrashic guise, that Lavan was even more insidious than Pharaoh. After all, Pharaoh sought to enslave, persecute, and even kill the Jewish people. But Lavan tried to prevent the Jewish people from ever coming into existence. Pharaoh tried to persecute us. Lavan tried to assimilate us.

In this context, note also the following *derashot*:

> **"And he sojourned there"**- this teaches that our father Jacob did not go down to Egypt to settle, but only to live there temporarily...
>
> **"And he became there a nation"**- this teaches that Israel was distinctive there.

Note that both of these paragraphs touch upon the issues in Yaakov's sojourn with Lavan, issues of survival and distinctiveness. When we go into exile, is it a periodic visit, or are we moving away on a permanent basis? This is precisely the issue that Yaakov struggled with against Lavan. Furthermore, how does one become a "nation"?

How does a small minority remain "distinct" whether in Mesopotamia or in Egypt? These are questions that go to the heart of survival as a people in Exile.

And now, the Haggada's "*derash*" comes into its true focus. In order to have the phrase "*Arami Oved Avi*" enlighten us on *Seder* night, it needs to be reshaped and understood in the perspective of the Exodus drama. It is about the attempted annihilation of the Jewish people. Arami– that Biblical personality known as Arami is now the character we know as Lavan. It is interesting that we don't even know Lavan's intentions in wanting Yaakov to stay. Maybe they were perfectly innocent! Maybe Lavan just wanted his daughters and grandchildren close at hand, not wanting to break up the family. And yet, we know that the act of remaining in Aram was a mistake that would have prevented the creation of the Jewish People, it would have undermined covenantal history, for the Children of Israel would never have come into being as a nation! Indeed, "Lavan sought to uproot everything!"

The Story Re-told: Why Bother?

Rabbi Ezra Labaton

The Haggada is a revered text. Family members gather around the Haggada on the first nights of Passover to plumb its wisdom and gather insights into our historical experience. As a people, this love of the Haggada text expresses itself in the multiple commentaries that Rabbis have authored over the centuries: Midrashic commentaries, Medieval commentaries, Rabbinic commentaries, Kabbalistic commentaries, Renaissance humanistic commentaries and of course Modern commentaries. A year does not go by without the publication of a new commentary on the Haggada. This year Rabbi Norman Lamm's commentary was just published, while last year Rabbi Soloveichick's commentary graced our table, gleaming with new ideas, thoughts and concepts. The pathways of Jewish creativity in reading and interpreting the Haggada seem endless. On a yearly basis the Haggada asks of us questions and expects newly minted creative answers. Or better, the Haggada asks of us – begs of us – to ask the questions ourselves and respond to these self imposed questions with answers of deeper understanding of what the Haggada tries to teach us.

On this holiday of questions, I raise my Passover question on precisely that Haggada passage that challenges us to study again and again, to raise new questions and provide new creative answers.

First, let us note that the Haggada begins by asking its famous four questions. Then, the Haggada answers these questions with the classic response of *Avadim*. For me, this very answer contains the seeds of my question. Here we read:

> "Even if we are all wise,
> And we are all understanding,

And we are all elders,
And we all know the Torah,
We are obligated to tell the story
Of the Exodus from Egypt"

I ask why? What is it the point of telling a story that we all know? We know the beginning, the middle and the end of the story. It's the same story as last year. Nothing new, nothing has changed. But the Haggada persists and emphasizes: Even if we are *Hachamim* (accumulated much knowledge), even if we are *Nevonim* (insightful), and even if we are *Zekenim* (we have been to the seder table many times before and the story has not changed!) – still we must retell. And again the question comes to the fore: Why must we re-tell a story that we all know?

Certainly, the most obvious answer is that we are not retelling the story for ourselves but for the children who asked the questions. This answer, however, has to be rejected for two reasons. A) Even if we are completely alone, and there are no children, still we must retell the story. B) The next paragraph of the five great Rabbis – who were all *Hachamim*, *Nevonim* and *Zekenim,* sitting among themselves - retold the story till the wee hours of the morning! Proof positive, that even the greatest Rabbis, who know all, still must still tell the story – even if they sit alone.

Ramban solves the enigma of why great Rabbis must re-tell a story that is already known to them by emphasizing the important role that the Exodus plays in our world view. In his commentary to Devarim (6:20-21), he elaborates on the *Avadim Hayinu* answer to the *Ki Yish'alecha Bincha* verse. Exodus teaches us about the infinite power of the Almighty and His sovereign mastery over the universe. *Yesi'at Misrayim* demonstrated this mastery over the natural order and we collectively as a nation witnessed this demonstration of Divine power. Our recognition of *Bore*

Olam is rooted in our collective experience and vicarious experience of the Exodus. The story must be re-told, if only to re-experience and deepen that awareness of the Sovereign master of all. The re-telling may not grant any new information – but it highlights how central this experience was for the Jewish people. After all, the Ramban argues, the Ten Commandments do not introduce *Bore Olam* not as He who created heaven and earth, but as He who took us out of Egypt. Further, the stated reason in *Devarim* for the holiday of Shabbat is *Yesi'at Misrayim*. Given this central role, the story must be re-told – no matter how wise we are or how many times we heard the story before.

Rabbi Soloveichick, in his Haggada commentary, raises the very same question. Why must great Rabbis re-tell a story well known to one and all? He roots his answer in the peculiar formulation of the Haggada itself. The Haggada says, מצוה עלינו לספר ביציאת מצרים- "we are commanded to tell the story of the Exodus." The more conventional way to express this thought would have been מצוה עלינו לספר את יציאת מצרים.

Rabbi Soloveichick explains the distinction between these two formulations. The latter (לספר את) refers to a fixed narrative, a story with clear demarcations: A beginning, middle and end. After the narrative is told and the details known, there is nothing more to say. The Haggada's formulation (לספר ביציאת מצרים), however, indicates more than a simple re-telling. Here the *mitzvah* is, "להעמיק בו ולהבינו על בריו ולא רק לספר את המעשה שהיה"— we are required to add dimensions to our knowledge of the story. The Haggada demands not a simple review of events that took place, but a deeper understanding of the theological and spiritual forces, as they intersected with the historical fact of the Exodus. That is, though the great Rabbis may know the simple story, they must deepen – from year to year – their understanding of this central event. Indeed, why the Almighty interacts within the historical process and when, is a profound philosophical question that even the greatest of Jewish minds must think about and revisit.

Here Rabbi Soloveichick is teaching us that our knowledge and understanding of *Bore Olam* should grow from year to year (presumably, after a year of more Torah study) and therefore we should be able to add new and deeper insights – every year. Rabbi Soloveichick demands of the story teller more than a simple re-telling of the story. He must deepen our understanding of the event, adding new dimensions each time the Mitza of *sippur* is engaged.

Leaving aside the Medieval commentary of the Ramban and the Modern commentary of Rabbi Soloveichick, one may analyze the Haggada's phrase from a Rabbinic contextual/literary point of view. We note that this formulation of "וכל המרבה...הרי זה משובח" ("the more that one does…the more praiseworthy it is") appears in only two other contexts in all of the vast ocean of Rabbinic literature. First, we find this formulation in the *Mishna* of Sanhedrin (5:1) Here, the judges of a capital case are told that the more they ask, the more they challenge - the more praiseworthy. The accused, about to be executed, may not be able to defend himself from the testimony of the two witnesses. Here the judges must take on the role of the defender of the accused and challenge the witnesses. After all, a person's life hangs in the balance. The judges must go beyond the pro forma questioning of the witnesses. The judges, through their challenges to the witnesses, will save a life - or not. Here, the *Mishna* demands of the judges to ask more, beyond the minimum, and even beyond the maximum, for the sake of the accused. And the judge who goes beyond – is praiseworthy.

A second formulation of this type is found in *Mo'ed Kattan* (Yerushalmi 18b). Here the *Gemara* declares that the more that one engages in the mourning rituals for his deceased parents deserves praise. The *Gemara* here is concerned with the proper honor due to the mourner's parents. The *Korban Edah* adds that the purpose of the "רבוי"- doing more honor to the deceased- is that it provides more comfort for the mourner. Indeed, the *hesped* based on this "רבוי" could give added significance and meaning to the life of the deceased which as well provides help to the mourner.

Do these three contexts, all of which have this very specific formulation – have anything in common? Can one shed light on another? Or, more specifically, do these two other Rabbinical contexts – with the same formulation as our Haggada – expand or enhance our understanding of the Haggada's formulation? Without overly eisegizing the matter, perhaps this unique formulation indicates that in the same way that a judge in a capital case can ask ordinary questions, and receive ordinary answers, so too a person telling the story of the Exodus can do so in an ordinary fashion – simply going through the motions. Or, the judge may seek out every nook and cranny, may challenge every detail, may bring the event to life through his incisive, penetrating, well-chosen words. Here the story teller is warned through this formulation that *Yesi'at Misrayim* must be told with the same zeal and passion, with the same concern and intensity, with the same penetrating insight, as a judge who sees the life of the accused in his hands. The judge and the story teller are both praised if they conduct themselves beyond the expected measure. The judge must interrogate properly, while he who tells the story of the Exodus must tell the story appropriately - learning the right lessons from the interrogating judge.

And the same is true for the mourner of parents who finds comfort in engaging in עסקיו של מת (the needs of the deceased), or for those who seek to comfort the mourner with a *hesped* that frames the life of the deceased in a way that helps the mourner deal with the tragedy. A *hesped* could be ordinary or pro forma, where the *maspid* fails to give meaning and a broader context to the life of the deceased. The mourners remain unmoved and uncomforted. The ordinary words spoken are insipid and empty of meaning. Or the *maspid,* through the power of the spoken word, can turn a tragic loss of sadness into a meaningful event that adds a dimension of significance to the life of the deceased, thereby helping the mourner work his way through the mass of emotions he feels at this loss.

Similarly, the narrative of the Exodus could be recited in an ordinary, run-of-the-mill fashion – adding neither depth, meaning, significance nor insight. The same story told as last year. Or, as the gifted *maspid*, the well chosen words of the story teller can re-create the narrative in a way that adds significance and meaning to the re-telling. The same participant as last year may grace the seder table and though he heard the very same story, sees it with greater clarity and greater insight. The narrative has been re-told in a fashion that has added a deeper dimension of understanding and is seen in a broader framework. In all these cases, the extra effort is praised. This literary analysis of the key Rabbinic phrase has indeed helped us understand why the known story of the Exodus has to be retold. The other two Rabbinic contexts added a dimension of understanding to the Haggada's formulation.

There is one final way of approaching a solution to the question, why must great Rabbis, who know the story, re-tell it? Simply, because words matter. Words convey more than knowledge. Words have the power of changing the speaker of the words – even when the speaker recites words which he has recited many times before. The speaker may be moved by his recitation of a narrative he knows – if the appropriate words are chosen – even if he learns nothing new with no new dimensions explored. These words – though recited many times before – penetrate his heart, mind and soul, stimulating a new spiritual response. Such is the power of the recited word.

Prayer may be a good analogy. Many have prayed the same words time and time again. In the last fifty two years that I have supplicated my Creator, not one word has changed. Yet, the words are still meaningful; they still have the power to move, stimulate, shock and even transform me. Admittedly, some days of prayer are better than others. But on the "better" days, the very same words that I have recited literally thousands of times before, can recharge an old spiritual battery. The Rabbis of the Talmud, who organized and chose these words of prayer, praise and thanksgiving, understood well the energizing power of the *Siddur*'s words. [For more on the power of Prayer, see Rabbi Eliezer's monograph on the "Art of Prayer", and R. Abraham Heschel's *Man in Search of God* – both works are wonderful expositions on the efficacy and life transforming power of prayer.]

The very same could be said of the Exodus narrative. The words themselves, though recited for years prior, still have the capacity to move and energize the story teller. Thus, even if alone, even if it's a story many times re-told, and even if the teller is the greatest of scholars – this time may be different. These very same words may serve to provide a spark of spiritual change in the teller of the narrative.

Or, put a bit differently, the *mitzvah* of "*Sippur Yesiat Misraim*," is not about new knowledge, new aspects, new dimensions or new insights. It's about creating a feeling of " בכל דור ודור חייב אדם לראות (להראות) את עצמו כאילו הוא יצא ממצרים", "in every generation a person is obligated to see himself as if he left Egypt." Admittedly, living in the lap of luxury as most of us, it's hard to imagine ourselves as slaves, serving the awesome Pharoah. Not so for the Jew subject to the flames of the Inquisition, Chmielnicki pogroms or concentration camp. They all saw themselves as living in compromised slave-like situations. For them the servitude was real, as were their prayers for redemption. We have a more difficult time with the notion of seeing ourselves as redeemed from Egypt. Yet, try we must. And the words of re-telling are there to create psychologically and emotionally- even momentarily - the experience of servitude and redemption.

Imagine that these words of the Exodus narrative have been told and retold thousands upon thousands of times, by millions upon millions of Jews, during the last two thousand years. The Jews who told and retold the story may have been wise, and aged, and may have heard this very same narrative many times before. Yet, they were always faithful to the *mitzvah* and once again retold the story. Either to emphasize its importance or to gain some new insight into Divine providence and how it operates within the historical context; Or, because the words had the power to change the story teller himself, or enable him to experience in some fashion or other, the servitude and redemption experienced by our forefathers. However we understand the *mitzvah* of *Sippur*, let us point out that it is the key to a meaningful Haggada experience. The *Ba'al HaHaggada* certainly knew how to stimulate the right questions, now we must take the challenge and find the right answers.

On Influencing the Future[1]

Rabbi Norman Lamm

It is an article of our faith that man has been endowed by his Creator with *behirah hofshit*, free will. He is permitted to make a free choice between right and wrong. In that sense, his future is open and undetermined. By opting for good or for evil, man can create his own destiny and fashion his own fate. "See, I have set before thee this day life and good, and death and evil, in that I command thee this day to love the Lord thy God, to walk in His ways...Therefore choose life, that thou mayest live, thou and thy seed" (*Nitzavim*, Deut. 30: 15-19).

And yet, for all that, the future is not *altogether* open and undetermined. The past does exert a powerful influence on the present, and through the present on the future. Heredity, for instance, plays a great role in the choices open to an individual. Some people are born stubborn, other more pliable; some lazy and some diligent; some rebellious and some obedient. Such facts limit our choice, although they do not by any means cancel it out altogether.

There are some such limiting factors that are the result of an initially free determination by man. For instance, take environment. The kind of society in which we live, the kind of friends we have, often determines what kind of life we shall lead. But we are free to choose our society and to select our friends. Therefore, if we choose for ourselves a corrupt society and the wrong sort of friends, we are in essence making a choice which will determine a great part of our future. If we opt for the right kind of environment,

---

[1] This essay was delivered on the 8th Day Passover, April 4th 1964, at The Jewish Center and was a fundraiser for Yeshiva University. It is reprinted here with some minor modifications. This essay and other essays by Dr. Lamm are available in his new Haggadah commentary, *The Royal Table* (OU Press, 2010).

then too we are creating our own future.

One of the most important factors in determining that future is – what we *think* of that future itself, how we visualize it, what we expect of it. What we consider the future will often determine what it will turn out to be. Our estimate of the future is frequently, in itself, an influence on that future.

Do you recall Shakespeare's immortal play, "Macbeth?" We meet the young victorious general as he returns from putting down a rebellion against the King. The King is grateful to this young soldier who has displayed such valorous loyalty. On the way back, in the famous scene on the heath, Macbeth meets the witches. We notice a malevolent change occurring in the character of Macbeth as he peeks into the future with the aid of witchcraft. This glimpse into the unknown, in which he is told that he will himself become King, redirects the development of his personality. We know that the witches' prophecies are, in essence, suggestions from Macbeth's own mind. We know that they are half-truths, which he wants to believe, for secretly he covets the throne for himself. Thus, his is a self-created future; because he believes that he will become King, he ultimately does – at the expense of his peace of mind, the purity of his character, and, ultimately, his very life. The faithful soldier has willed himself into the future of a perfidious rebel. What the poet is telling us is that man often becomes what he chooses to believe about himself.

> "It hath been taught us from the primal state
> That he which is was wished until he were."

Shakespeare is teaching us a universal principle: that what we wish will come; that things happen often because we expect them to happen; that the vision of the future is at least as powerful as the facts of the past in shaping our own destinies.

This is true of men and it is true of societies. Inspect

their dreams and you will discover their future. A brutal ideology, which tolerates inhumanity and accepts the lawlessness of the jungle – whether it be Nazism or Fascism or a primitive evolutionism – will breed that very kind of society. A man who considers himself only a complicated machine, without real meaning or purpose in life, will become just that: a cipher, a statistic, a helpless plastic lump of humanity that is molded by external forces and without an inner will, an ineffective man or woman who cannot control his own destiny—in short, a nobody.

But if the dreams are of the reverse kind, if the expectation of the future and the estimate of his self is that of one who considers himself a living, loving, feeling, thinking, free being, one created in the *tzellem Elokim*, and therefore utterly unique – such a person will become just that: a purposeful, thoughtful, free, unique, and distinct individual in his own rights.

These last days of Passover we read the *shirah*, the Song of Triumph at the shores of the Red Sea. Immediately before the beginning of the song, we read the immortal words *va-yaaminu ba-Shem u-ve'Mosheh avdo*, the Children of Israel believed in the Lord and in His servant Moses. Somehow, it seems, the Torah was trying to tell us that a relationship exists between the belief and the triumph. Indeed, our Sages taught: *lo nig'alu Yisrael mi-Mitzrayim ela bi'sekhar emunah*, Israel was redeemed from Egypt for the faith they had.

Do the Rabbis mean to teach us that there was a simple trade, a kind of barter as a form of reward-and-punishment?—that the immediate wages of faith or *emunah* are redemption or *ge'ulah*?

I believe not. Our Sages were not speaking of faith in its purely theological context, such as faith in the existence or unity of God. I believe that what they meant is that the *faith in the redemption* itself brought on the redemption! The confidence that Israel had in the future determined that future. The *ge'ulah* came about as the result of Israel's *emunah* in its own *ge'ulah*.

In a similar vein, the rabbis promised that *ein ha-galuyot mitkansim ela bi'sekhar emunah*, the in-gathering of the exiles in the days before Messiah will come about in return for the faith of Israel. Think back to the years before 1948, when our contemporary *kibbutz galuyot* or in-gathering of the exiles began. At that time it took a tremendous amount of courage to believe that it was possible for the straggling remnants of European Jewry to form an independent state and return to Zion. Those who entertained such visions were accused of dreaming pipe-dreams and flirting with dangerous hallucinations. Yet those who maintained a dogged faith in this vision lived to see it. Our very faith was itself instrumental in achieving it. Indeed, the future tends to conform to your opinion of it.

> "It hath been taught us from the primal state
> That he which is was wished until he were."

People sometimes wonder: why is it that, by and large, our people are *rahamanim*, compassionate and merciful, with liberal tendencies, and generally in favor of human rights for all. Even when you meet a segregationist Jew, you usually find that he is more moderate and humane than others, disposed towards decent treatment to the very people he may oppose. What accounts for this? In all probability it is: our vision of the future! Read today's haftarah – Isaiah's picture of the Messiah and his period – and you will see how our vision of the future has indelibly impressed itself upon our present and directed us to a certain kind of character. Not for us the dreams of drunken power, lording it over others who remain permanently inferior and subordinate. Instead, we dream of a Messiah who will judge the poor in justice, of a world of universal peace in which natural enemies will live together, the lamb with the wolf, the kid with the leopard. Our dream is one of universal knowledge – "for the world will be filled with the knowledge of the Lord even as the waters cover the sea." For a people, even as for an individual, "he which is was wished until he were!"

What kind of future do we American Orthodox Jews dream of for ourselves and our children in this country? I would define it as follows: on the one hand, we want to have a community of Jews who will be loyal to Judaism and to the Jewish tradition; dedicated to the people of Israel and to the State of Israel; who will produce individual *talmidei ḥakhamim*, and a generation which will be a *dor dei'ah*, knowledgeable and versed in Torah. And on the other hand, we want them to be creative members of American society; fully cultured and conversant with all aspects of Western civilization; leaders in their professions and careers, assuming the leadership of the Jewish community and the community at large. But above all, we want to be able to merge both worlds, to combine both disciplines, to synthesize both traditions.

Do you recognize that dream, one which we hope will in and of itself guide us towards that kind of future? If we had to describe that dream in two words, they would be "Yeshiva University!" Yeshiva, with its intensive schools of Jewish learning and education, and its excellent secular department where subjects ranging from medicine and science through the liberal arts are taught from the high school to the post-graduate and post-doctoral level, supplies the generation of the future with the materials and the stuff by which our dreams can be transformed into reality.

Yeshiva University is not only an institution. It is a faith, a vision, a dream, a destiny. Do not underestimate it. I have seen Jews on three continents inspired to new heights when they hear the details about this most significant of all Jewish institutions of modern times. Yeshiva University is that definition of ourselves that tells us what we *can* become.

But we must beware of merely wishing ourselves into a better future. We must be careful lest we resort merely to an infantile kind of wish-fulfillment. What I propose is not a childish conception whereby if you want a thing strongly enough, the very wish will bring it about; but rather that kind of faith and optimism that elicits from us work, dedication, and endless effort and endeavor.

I beg you to remember that the Rabbis promised the *ge'ulah*, the ultimate redemption, as *sekhar emunah*. That last phrase should not be understood as "the reward for faith," but in a different sense altogether. For the word *sekhar* means not only reward, something given in return, but also: compensation, payment, a kind of deposit. The redemption came about not as a reward for faith, but as a result of *sekhar emunah* – the effort, the work, the payment that was offered because of *emunah*, the faith in the vision. It is not enough to have *emunah*; one must also add his *sekhar*. If we are willing to give, to pledge, to pay, as an expression of our faith, then indeed we will be privileged to experience the *ge'ulah,* the kind of redemption which will restore us not only to our national home, but to our national destiny — the return of the People of Israel to the Land of Israel according to the Torah of Israel. For this is indeed the final redemption itself, the *ge'ulah shelemah*.

Come Let Us Deal Shrewdly With Them[1]

Nehama Leibowitz

וַיֹּאמֶר, אֶל-עַמּוֹ:
הִנֵּה, עַם בְּנֵי יִשְׂרָאֵל רַב וְעָצוּם מִמֶּנּוּ
הָבָה נִתְחַכְּמָה לוֹ,
פֶּן-יִרְבֶּה
וְהָיָה כִּי-תִקְרֶאנָה מִלְחָמָה
וְנוֹסַף גַּם-הוּא עַל-שֹׂנְאֵינוּ,
וְנִלְחַם-בָּנוּ, וְעָלָה מִן-הָאָרֶץ.

He said to his people,
Look, the Israelite people have become too
many and too strong for us.
Come, let us deal shrewdly with them
Lest they increase
And if war breaks out they will join our enemies
And fight against us and leave the country.

(1:9-10)

The above passage admittedly expresses Pharaoh's desire to solve his "Jewish problem." But his precise intentions are by no means clear. Pharaoh possibly at this juncture was not himself sure as to what he intended to do, or perhaps he wished to conceal his intentions from his cabinet. Did he wish to limit the natural increase of the Israelites or to eliminate them entirely? Did he wish to enslave and exploit them or get rid of them so that they should not constitute a fifth column ready to join an outside enemy?

The first verse clearly complains of their threatening increase in numbers and power. But we must be careful not to treat the *mi* of *mimenu* as connoting "more than" as

---

[1] This study, reprinted from "New Studies in Shemot," was written for *parashat Shemot*. The verses quoted in the beginning of this study-which are the topic of discussion - are recited in the Haggadah.

many non-Jewish Bible translators from the Septuagint and Vulgate onwards have done. He does not mean that the children of Israel were greater in number and power *than* the Egyptians. But rather, as the Jewish translators Mendelssohn, Hirsch, Buber-Rosenzweig, and some modern English versions have it: "they are too many and too powerful *for us*." The "*mem*" is one of relativeness. They are getting too many for us to cope with.

But the second verse is puzzling: "Come let us deal shrewdly with them." Why did Pharaoh the ruler of the Egyptian empire require to look for pretexts "to deal wisely" with the helpless Jewish minority in his realm? Why could he not destroy them by fire and sword without further ado? Who was to gainsay him? Here is Ramban's answer detailing Pharaoh's policy stage by stage:

> Pharaoh and his advisers did not regard it as a wise step to put the Israelites to the sword; for this would have constituted rank treason to persecute without cause a people that had come to the land at the bidding of his royal predecessor. Moreover, the people of the land would not have allowed the king to commit this violence since he had to consult them. All the more so in view of the fact that the Children of Israel were a mighty and numerous people who would make war with them. Later, he suggested looking for a device by which the Israelites should not feel that any hostile act was being committed against them. For this reason, he imposed on them a tax; for it was the custom of strangers in a country to pay a tax to the king. Afterwards, he secretly ordered the midwives to put to death the male children on the birthstools when even the mothers themselves did not know what was going on. Then he commanded all of his people that they should cast every male child into the river. He did not give such an order to his chief executioners to slay them by the sword at the royal bidding or to cast them into the river,

but he told the people to do so, and that if the father of the child were to protest to the king or his representative they should ask him to bring evidence to substantiate his accusation and for vengeance to be done. And when the king allowed matters to take their course, the Egyptians searched Jewish homes and even took the children from there. That is the implication of the statement "and they could no longer hide him."

Ramban proposes three reasons for Pharaoh's policy of not declaring open war on Israel. First, it would be "rank treason to smite without cause a people that had come to the land at the bidding of his royal predecessor." Even the most corrupt ruler cannot suddenly exterminate a people without a shadow of a pretext. There must be some semblance of justice if only to satisfy his own conscience. What would other countries say? Second, his own subjects would not agree. He had to consult them first. Internal public opinion must be placated. He could not suddenly order the indiscriminate slaughter of persons who have been good neighbors for so long (they borrowed from each other domestic utensils…).

Third, the Israelites themselves were "mighty and numerous and would make war with them." They would not go like lambs to the slaughter but would defend themselves. Even if he was sure his army could crush them—why risk such an unnecessary confrontation. Rather "Let us deal shrewdly with them," so that "the Israelites should not feel that any hostile act was being committed against them." Pharaoh, King of Egypt, the cradle of civilization, science and art, could not exterminate innocent people.

Ramban outlines the stages of Pharaoh's policy. First a tax on foreigners—not of money but of labor—which was customary. If the labor exceeded the bounds of the humane, who was to measure it? If the victims complained, the accusation of: "you are lazy, you are lazy" (5:17) could always be hurled at them. Since slavery, however ruthless, would not be the "final solution," he advocated facilitating the process by the killing of the male children at birth by the midwives when "even the mothers would not know what was going on." Even if suspicion was aroused as a result of the enormous rise in male child mortality, who would be able or dare to point an accusing finger at Pharaoh? Only when the heroism of the midwives foiled his plan did he come out into the open and "commanded all his people" to kill every male child.

The originality of Ramban's interpretation lies in his explanation of this command. The text states that Pharaoh commanded "all his people" rather than "his princes and servants." This was not therefore an official royal edict, but behind-the-scenes provocation. The government gave no order but merely closed its eyes whilst the Egyptian masses "spontaneously" vented their indignation on the foreigners. Although Egyptian law protected strangers, in practice there would be no redress. The situation would be just as Ramban outlined:

> And when the king allowed matters to take their course the Egyptians searched Jewish homes and even took the children from there. That is the implication of the statement "and they could no longer hide him."

They no longer waited to chance upon a Jewish infant hidden by the banks of the Nile but "searched Jewish homes." They went further than Pharoah's command. Accordingly when the matter got out-of-hand the decree was suspended:

> Evidently this state of affairs lasted for a short time only, since when Aaron was born the decree was not in force. Apparently, immediately after the birth of Moses it was already withdrawn. Perhaps Pharaoh's daughter in her compassion for him had besought her father not

to carry it out. Or when it was heard that such was the desire of the king it was abolished.

This explanation solves a further difficulty involved in Pharaoh's policy. When the Israelite overseers left Pharaoh after failing to persuade him to alleviate the bondage they complained to Moses and Aaron:

‎---יֵרֶא יְהוָה עֲלֵיכֶם וְיִשְׁפֹּט,
‎אֲשֶׁר הִבְאַשְׁתֶּם אֶת-רֵיחֵנוּ בְּעֵינֵי פַרְעֹה וּבְעֵינֵי עֲבָדָיו,
‎לָתֶת-חֶרֶב בְּיָדָם לְהָרְגֵנוּ.

May the Lord look upon you and judge
How you have discredited us in the eyes of
Pharaoh and his subjects.

(5:21)

Surely was it only at this juncture after Moses and Aaron had come to Pharaoh with the demand: "Let my people go" that the Egyptians had begun to threaten Jewish life? Surely they had thrown their children into the Nile? But Ramban's explanation solves this difficulty. Hitherto Pharaoh had not openly declared war on them. "It would have constituted rank treason to persecute without cause." But once the seeds of rebellion and dissatisfaction began to sprout in the shape of such revolutionary slogans as "let us go and sacrifice to the Lord our God," "let my people go" the situation was different. Pharaoh could openly challenge them:

This explains the force of Moses' statement to the Almighty that "You have discredited us in the eyes of Pharaoh... to put a sword in their hand...." The Egyptians would now continue to hate us and use it as a pretext that we were rebelling against the government. They would be able to kill us with the sword publicly, and would have no need to use indirect methods.

81

This is therefore Ramban's explanation of the phrase: "let us deal shrewdly with them" giving us to understand why Pharaoh had to use indirect, devious methods in destroying the Jewish people.

Unlike Rashi who gives a "localized" explanation – one confined to the point arising out of the actual text he is commenting on, Ramban often appends a "comprehensive" one which solves a number of difficulties that extend over a chapter or more. Why did Pharaoh approach the midwives? Why did he command his people rather than his officers and ministers? Why is there no mention of the decree against the male children after Moses' birth? Why did not Aaron's birth involve danger? Why did the overseers accuse Moses and Aaron of putting a sword in the hands of their oppressors? Characteristically, Ramban provides an answer to all these questions at one fell swoop in his detailed presentation of Pharaoh's policy of camouflage and deceit.

Questions for Further Study:

1. Which verse in Shemot would seem to contradict Ramban's assumption that Pharaoh's decrees were unofficial, underground and provocative rather than official published edict?

2. Does Ramban's explanation of verse 11 below fit in with the one he gives to the previous verse which formed the subject of our study?

> *"overseers to afflict him"*: He imposed a tax on the people in the form of labor in the king's service. Egyptian officials were appointed to mobilize the labor force in whatever way they wished. They were to work for a month or more on the royal buildings and then were allowed home. In this way "they built store cities for Pharaoh." When this failed to break the spirit of the people the Egyptian ministers grew impatient and

decreed that any Egyptian could enslave any Jew he wished to do his work. This is the force of the text: "The Egyptians worked the children of Israel ruthlessly," They continued to step up their harassing tactics. Originally, the Israelites were provided by the state with the building material. Subsequently they had to go and search for their own. The labor was no longer confined to building but to any job of the most menial and arduous kind accompanied by lashes and curses. That is the force of the text: "in all manner of work with which they worked them ruthlessly." The king provided them with rations as customary with forced labor. This also explains the complaint made by the murmurers in the desert when they "remembered the fish we ate in Egypt, for nothing - the cucumbers...." For fish was plentiful in Egypt and they would take it from the fishermen in the royal service and also take the cucumbers and melons from the gardens and with no one to gainsay them, for so was the command of the king.

3. *Ve'ala min ha-arez* (literally: "he (i.e. Israel) shall go up out of the country" (1: 10).

על כרחנו ; ורבותינו דרשו : כאדם שמקלל עצמו ותולה קללתו באחרים והרי הוא כאילו כתב "ועלינו מן הארץ," והם יירשוה.

Against our will. But our Rabbis interpreted differently. They compared it to a person who wishes to curse himself but (euphemistically) attaches the curse to others. We are therefore to read the text as if it were written "then *we* shall have to leave the country" and they (the Israelites) will take over [cf. NEB: "they will become master of the country"].

(Rashi)

We may take it to mean that in the event of war the Israelites will join forces with the enemy to plunder and leave the country and return to Canaan with all our wealth

and we shall be unable to retaliate and fight back. Cf.
Exodus 32: 1; Jeremiah 23: 8; Hosea 2:2.

(Ramban)

a) What difficulty does the text (1:10) present?
b) Why was not Rashi satisfied with his first explanation but chose to add the rabbinic exposition?
c) Ramban solves the difficulty by adding one Hebrew word to the text. Which is it?

Miracles[1]

Rabbi Jonathan Sacks

The division of the Reed Sea is engraved in Jewish memory. We recite it daily in the morning service, at the transition from the Verses of Praise to the beginning of communal prayer. We speak of it again after the Shema, just before the Amidah. It was the supreme miracle of the exodus.

But in what sense? If we listen carefully to the narratives, we can distinguish two perspectives. This is the first:

> The waters were divided, and the Israelites went through the sea on dry ground, with *a wall of water* on their right and on their left . . . The water flowed back and covered the chariots and horsemen – the entire army of Pharaoh that had followed the Israelites into the sea. Not one of them survived. But the Israelites went through the sea on dry ground, with *a wall of water on their right and on their left.* (Exodus 14: 22, 28-29)

The same note is struck in the Song at the Sea:

> By the blast of Your nostrils
> The waters piled up.
> The surging waters stood firm like a wall;
> The deep waters congealed in the heart of the sea.
> (Exodus 15:8)

The emphasis here is on the supernatural dimension of what happened. Water, which normally flows, stood upright. The sea parted to expose dry land. The laws of

---

[1] This article is reprinted (with permission) from Rabbi Sacks' weekly parasha studies: *Covenant and Conversation.* It was written for *Parashat Beshallah* (5770), part of which is read on the 7th day of Passover.

nature were suspended. Something happened for which there can be no scientific explanation.

However, if we listen carefully, we can also hear a different note:

> Then Moses stretched out his hand over the sea, and *all that night the Lord drove the sea back with a strong east wind* and turned it into dry land. (Exodus 14: 21)

Here there is not a sudden change in the behavior of water, with no apparent cause. G-d brings a wind that, in the course of several hours, drives the waters back. Or consider this passage:

> During the last watch of the night the Lord looked down from the pillar of fire and cloud at the Egyptian army and threw it into confusion. *He made the wheels of their chariots come off so that they had difficulty driving.* The Egyptians said, "Let's get away from the Israelites! The Lord is fighting for them against Egypt." (Exodus 14: 24-25)

The emphasis here is less on miracle than on irony. The great military assets of the Egyptians – making them almost invulnerable in their day – were their horses and chariots. These were Egypt's specialty. They still were, in the time of Solomon, five centuries later:

> Solomon accumulated chariots and horses; he had fourteen hundred chariots and twelve thousand horses, which he kept in the chariot cities and also with him in Jerusalem . . . They imported a chariot from Egypt for six hundred shekels of silver, and a horse for a hundred and fifty. (I Kings 10: 26-29)

Viewed from this perspective, the events that took place could be described as follows: The Israelites had arrived at the Reed Sea at a point at which it was shallow. Possibly there was a ridge in the sea bed, normally covered by water, but occasionally – when, for example, a fierce east wind blows – exposed. This is how the Cambridge University physicist Colin Humphreys puts it in his recent book *The Miracles of Exodus* (2003):

> Wind tides are well known to oceanographers. For example, a strong wind blowing along Lake Erie, one of the Great Lakes, has produced water elevation differences of as much as sixteen feet between Toledo, Ohio, on the west, and Buffalo, New York, on the east...There are reports that Napoleon was almost killed by a "sudden high tide" while he was crossing shallow water near the head of the Gulf of Suez. (pp. 247-48)

In the case of the wind that exposed the ridge in the bed of the sea, the consequences were dramatic. Suddenly the Israelites, traveling on foot, had an immense advantage over the Egyptian chariots that were pursuing them. Their wheels became stuck in the mud. The charioteers made ferocious efforts to free them, only to find that they quickly became mired again. The Egyptian army could neither advance nor retreat. So intent were they on the trapped wheels, and so reluctant were they to abandon their prized war machines, the chariots, that they failed to notice that the wind had dropped and the water was returning. By the time they realized what was happening, they were trapped. The ridge was now covered with sea water in either direction, and the island of dry land in the middle was shrinking by the minute. The mightiest army of the ancient world was defeated, and its warriors drowned, not by a superior army, not by human opposition at all, but by its own folly in being so focused on capturing the Israelites that they ignored the fact that they were driving into mud where their chariots could not go.

We have here two ways of seeing the same events: one natural, the other supernatural. The supernatural explanation – that the waters stood upright – is immensely powerful, and so it entered Jewish memory. But the natural explanation is no less compelling. The Egyptian strength proved to be their weakness. The weakness of the Israelites became their strength. On this reading, what was significant was less the supernatural than the moral dimension of what happened. G-d visits the sins on the sinners. He mocks those who mock Him. He showed the Egyptian army, which reveled in its might, that the weak were stronger than they – just as He later did with the pagan prophet Bilaam, who prided himself in his prophetic powers and was then shown that his donkey (who could see the angel Balaam could not see) was a better prophet than he was.

To put it another way: a miracle is not necessarily something that suspends natural law. It is, rather, an event for which there may be a natural explanation, but which – happening when, where and how it did – evokes wonder, such that even the most hardened sceptic senses that G-d has intervened in history. The weak are saved; those in danger, delivered. More significantly still is the moral message such an event conveys: that hubris is punished by nemesis; that the proud are humbled and the humble given pride; that there is justice in history, often hidden but sometimes gloriously revealed.

Not all Jewish thinkers focused on the supernatural dimension of G-d's involvement in human history. Maimonides, for example, writes:

> The Israelites did not believe in Moses our teacher because of the miraculous signs he performed. When someone's faith is founded on miraculous signs, there is always a lingering doubt in the mind that these signs may have been performed with magic or witchcraft. All the signs Moses performed in the wilderness, he did because they were necessary, not to establish his credentials as a prophet. (*Mishneh Torah, Hilkhot Yesodei ha-Torah*, 8:1)

What made Moses the greatest of the prophets, says Maimonides, it not that he performed supernatural deeds but that, at Mount Sinai, he brought the people the word of G-d.

Nachmanides, with a somewhat different approach, emphasizes the phenomenon he calls a "hidden miracle", an event that, though consistent with the laws of nature, is no less wondrous: the existence of the universe, the fact that we are here, the sustenance and shelter with which we are provided, and so on. "G-d", said Einstein, "does not play dice with the universe." The astonishing complexity of life, and the sheer improbability of existence (nowadays known as the anthropic principle), are miracles *disclosed* by science, not challenged by science.

The genius of the biblical narrative of the crossing of the Reed Sea is that it does not resolve the issue one way or another. It gives us both perspectives. To some the miracle was the suspension of the laws of nature. To others, the fact that there was a naturalistic explanation did not make the event any less miraculous. That the Israelites should arrive at the sea precisely where the waters were unexpectedly shallow, that a strong east wind should blow when and how it did, and that the Egyptians' greatest military asset should have proved their undoing – all these things were wonders, and we have never forgotten them.

Reflections on Passover[1]

Rabbi Moshe Shamah

1. Uniqueness of the Exodus

The Torah's account of G-d's redemption of Israel from Egyptian bondage is part of a much larger story, intrinsically connected with the Covenant that G-d established with the patriarchs and His long-term agenda for human society. The Israelite's liberation should not be thought of as a successful "national liberation movement," comparable to those events in history when people fought for and succeeded in gaining their freedom. True, the Passover narrative has often inspired the oppressed and downtrodden, as well it should, encouraging them to hope and strive for deliverance from tyranny. The humbling of a mighty, wicked and stubborn ruler; his helplessness in the face of Divine visitations of plagues; and his ultimately being rendered pathetic in defeat are surely among the most pleasing images imaginable to a subjugated populace. The same may be said of reading about an oppressed and suffering people marching to their freedom and destiny, carrying off some of the riches of their erstwhile masters, as beautifully depicted in the Torah.

But the Exodus from Egypt was neither a grassroots revolution nor one fomented by dynamic leaders. This is made crystalclear in the narrative and is an important feature of the essential message. The narrative cannot be severed from the unique context in which it is deeply embedded without losing the essence of the biblical message.

---

[1] The following study is reprinted from Rabbi Shamah's weekly parasha studies, and was written for the section of *Parashat Bo* that is read on the First Day of Passover.

Moshe, Israel's emerging leader, was extraordinarily sensitive to the plight of his brethren from his earliest days, keenly interested in justice for them as well as for all other people. He was courageous and energetic. He was willing to personally intervene (perhaps somewhat impulsively) at the risk of his own welfare and even his life; he was willing to jeopardize his princely position in the palace in order to rescue a single victim of the harsh slavery. He also tried to correct what he perceived to be wrongful behavior among his brethren. But the Torah demonstrates that he could not get very far on his own. It is also evident that this gifted individual, the humblest of men, possessed neither the driving personal ambition nor confidence in his ability to play the organizer's role – traits that are typical of national liberation heroes. After barely escaping from Egypt with his life he resigned himself to a lengthy absence from his people. Hashem had to prod and press him and help him overcome his feelings of inadequacy in order to get him to accept the mission to return to Egypt to work toward his nation's liberation as Hashem's representative.

The established leaders of the Israelites had resigned themselves to their fate as slaves. After Moshe's first audience with Pharaoh, when the slavery was intensified, those leaders bitterly criticized him for his activities and exhibited no interest in fighting for their rights. At that point Moshe complained to Hashem: "Why did You send me? Ever since I came to Pharaoh to speak in Your name, he has dealt worse with this people" (Exod. 5:22-23). When he presented an inspiring message from Hashem to the Israelites, they paid no heed to it because of their circumstances. Even after their departure from Egypt, when they were being pursued by their former masters, they would not mobilize to protect their newly gained independence. Rather, they complained to Moshe, "Is this not what we told you in Egypt, saying, leave us alone and we will serve the Egyptians, for we prefer to serve the

Egyptians than to die in the desert?" (Exod. 14:12). On their own, the Israelites were unwilling to risk a possible deterioration of their situation to advance what appeared to be the far-fetched prospect of liberty.

G-d redeemed the Israelites in order to take the children of the meritorious patriarchs as His people, enter into a Covenant with them and create a nation that ultimately will bring blessing to the world. He expressed His purpose at the time of His selection of Abraham: "And I will make you a great nation…and all the families of the earth will be blessed through you" (Gen. 12:2-3); He elaborated on His reason in a declaration He made concerning Abraham: "And all the nations of the earth shall be blessed through him, for I know him that he will instruct his children and household after him to observe the way of Hashem to do righteousness and justice in the world" (Gen. 18:17-19). The "way of Hashem" is expanded upon in related assertions, such as "Only in this shall one pride himself, that he perceives and understands Me, that I, Hashem, act with kindness, justice and righteousness on earth, for in these do I desire" (Jer. 9:23). At a point when the Israelites cried out in their suffering under the yoke of oppression (Exod. 3:7) He deemed the time right to fulfill His commitment made to the patriarchs and began the process of their redemption (6:5-7).

Without G-d's direct involvement each step of the way there would have been no progress toward freedom either by the Israelites or their leaders. Hashem is the true "hero" of the story and His faithfulness and concern for Israel and human society are evident throughout.

Israel's slavery and attendant affliction are described in the Torah as preordained, at least to some degree. G-d revealed these details to Abraham before he had children, at the time He contracted with him the *berit ben habetarim* ("the Covenant of the Parts" [Gen. 15:13-16]). It was necessary for Abraham to know what he was getting his progeny into. We may assume that having the experience of painful oppression etched into the national consciousness of Israel helped nurture in it the extraordinary degree of sensitivity to the plight of the exploited and underprivileged that Torah law requires. The Lawgiving explicitly refers to remembering the slavery in Egypt as a motivational factor toward fulfillment of a number of laws that prescribe treating the widow, the orphan, the stranger, the slave – in general the poor and underprivileged – with fairness and decency. This sense of compassion and concern for others, together with the recognition that national redemption had been brought about through G-d's intervention for His purpose of establishing such a nation, were concepts that served as fundamental underlying motifs of the monumental venture.

The Torah relates that an additional purpose of the Exodus events was to bring to the world's awareness the existence of the one supreme, all-powerful G-d. He was making His omnipotent presence known through Israel, demonstrating that all natural forces are at His disposal. The mighty Egyptian nation, possessing one of the foremost cultures of the ancient world that had already been and would continue to be a great influence on civilizations, equipped with a prodigious military feared throughout the region, is forced to experience overpowering Divine intervention on behalf of Israel. The plagues, in their overall design and purpose, as well as the splitting of the sea, pointed to the one G-d who is the Author of creation, who is patient, preferring the reformation of sinners and who is concerned about humanity's appreciation of His reality. The wonders were intended to teach about His incomparability and the vanity of belief in other Divine beings. G-d articulated His purpose to Pharaoh after the sixth plague: "For this time I will send all My plagues to your heart, and at your servants and your people, in order that you shall know that there is none like Me in all the earth...For the following reason I have let you stand, to show you My power, and in order that My name will related throughout the earth" (Exod. 9:14-16). An opportunity was presented to the Egyptians and to all who heard of the extraordinary events to begin the process of subduing their idolatrous beliefs and practices.

2. Basic Principles

The redemption-covenant linkage had far-reaching consequences. Israel's existence as a nation is dependent on Hashem's special and continual intervention on its behalf. This reality is symbolized in its formative stage in Abraham and the barren Sarah having Isaac after her childbearing years had unquestionably passed and as made clear in events throughout the book of Genesis. In the natural order, Israel could not exist. Hence, it is summoned to order its society, as well as each individual member his personal life, in accordance with its founding identity of being Hashem's people and commanded to follow His law. In order to emphasize this point the Exodus leads directly and immediately to the Lawgiving in the wilderness even before entering the Promised Land. Indeed, Hashem had informed Moshe at the very initiation of his mission at the burning bush that the Exodus will straightaway lead to Mount Sinai: "When you have taken the people out of Egypt you (plural) will worship G-d on this mountain" (Exod. 3:12).

The Promised Land is an extremely important element in the Divine plan; it is where the nation may blossom, applying the values and particulars of the Torah unencumbered by foreign pressures and distractions. It is the arena, located at the crossroads of great empires, where the Divinely ordained system of holy living and social justice was expected to create a showcase that other nations may choose to emulate: "And many peoples shall go and say: 'Come, let us go up to the mount of the Lord, to the House of the G-d of Jacob, that He may teach us of His ways and that we may walk in His paths'" (Isa. 2:3). However, the land does not essentially define the nation. The covenantal relationship, with the Decalogue and the Mount Sinai experience at its core, was established in the wilderness and is the fundamental theme that runs through the Bible and underlies the nation's early history and destiny.

The implications of the wondrous events of the Exodus concerning the future are clear. The celebration of Passover calls upon the nation not to merely commemorate events of the past but to also reflect upon and appreciate what can be done at any time and in any situation. It summons the nation to be inspired by G-d's past intervention and work toward deserving His redeeming involvement in resolving whatever trouble may obtain.

Regarding the national exile in the days of Jeremiah, the prophet quotes Hashem concerning the future. The coming redemption will be so extraordinary that in that time "It shall no longer be said 'As Hashem lives who brought up the Israelites from the land of Egypt,' but rather, 'as Hashem lives who brought up the Israelites from the land of the north, and from all the lands to which He had cast them.' And I will bring them back to their land, which I gave to their fathers." (Jer. 16:14-15; also in 23:7 with slight variations). Just as during the Egyptian bondage, when the time was right in His sight, G-d overrode all obstacles to redeem His people and bring them to the Promised Land, at which time they would exercise their free will to properly accept His governance, He would once again reconfigure the cosmos to provide salvation and rejuvenation to His people and reestablish them in the Promised Land. That is the nature of a Covenant with G-d – anything is possible and everything depends on the commitment to fulfill His will.

As the Exodus comprises the founding event of the Israelites' national existence, its basic lessons were meant to apply throughout the generations to the nation as well as to each individual. Psalm 107 addresses the situation. It begins with citing the requirement for those redeemed in an ingathering of the exiles to give thanks and praise to G-d. It then turns to four successive cases of individuals who experienced various mortal dangers in their lives and who cried out to G-d, and whom He redeemed from their plight. The psalm elaborates on their requirement to give thankful praise to Him for the event they experienced as well as for other wonders He performed. As this psalm appears to carry forward an aspect of the lesson of the redemption from Egypt, it is fitting that the tradition prescribes it for daily recital during the days of Passover.

3. The Calendar

The first law promulgated as a consequence of the redemption from Egypt is הַחֹדֶשׁ הַזֶּה לָכֶם רֹאשׁ חֳדָשִׁים ("This month shall be for you the beginning of months" [Exod. 12:2]), that is, to henceforth count the month of the Exodus as the first month of the year in the national calendar. In this way the calendar gives prominence to the great event and reflects the fact that G-d's redemption is at the foundation of the nation. Moshe made a specific point of emphasizing the timing, "This day you are leaving is in the month of *abib*" (13:4), the month of spring (אָבִיב: ripening barley). This, in turn, coordinates the Passover message of national rejuvenation and hope with the great reawakening that all of nature undergoes with the coming of spring. G-d regulated His intervention such that the Exodus coincided with spring.

The passage in Deuteronomy that mandates the Passover commemoration begins with שָׁמוֹר אֶת חֹדֶשׁ הָאָבִיב וְעָשִׂיתָ פֶּסַח ("Guard the spring month and perform the

Pesaḥ" [Deut. 16:1]). This clearly prescribes (or reinforces) the requirement to focus on the Passover linkage with the spring month. The sages expounded this as a cornerstone requirement of the calendar: Passover must always fall during the spring month (the month within which the spring equinox occurs). Months (actual months, reflecting an astronomical phenomena) are lunar and Passover's dates (the sacrifice on the fourteenth of the first month and the festival beginning on the fifteenth) are lunar dates. It is thus necessary to establish a mechanism within the calendar to ensure that year after year the lunar date recurs in the same season despite the fact that seasons are determined by the solar cycle. This requires an intercalation between the years of the sun and the months of the moon. We will take this opportunity to provide some details about the Jewish calendar.

Months are functions of the moon's orbit and all Torah festivals are dated by it. (Since in the solar calendar months do not correspond to any astronomical phenomena but are merely conventional contrivances, they play no role in the Torah scheme of things.) Seasons, on the other hand, result from the sun's orbit. As lunar months are twenty-nine days, twelve hours, forty-four minutes and several seconds each, twelve lunar months comprise 354.37 days. A solar year is slightly longer than 365.24 days. In just a few "years" of twelve lunar months each (in a manner of speaking, as a true year is only a solar phenomenon), Passover would have drifted backwards relative to the seasons and occur in the winter and continually move backwards through the seasons. To ensure its falling in the spring, the solar and lunar calendars are merged such that an extra month is periodically added (intercalated) to the lunar "year" to compensate for the difference between cycles.

Originally, intercalation was based on astronomical calculation together with direct observation of the signs of spring. Early talmudic sages checked the state of the crops toward the end of winter and relied on the weather to determine if an adjustment (adding an extra month) had to be made in a particular year. As the primary purpose of adding a "leap" month is to ensure that Passover remain in the spring month (Nissan), it is added just before Passover's month, that is, to the twelfth month (Adar), and is called the Second Adar. By later talmudic times until the present day, however, intercalation has been determined strictly by calculation.

The calendar is now structured such that the twenty-nine and a half days of each lunar cycle are resolved into months of either twenty-nine or thirty days each, with no exceptions. In a "regular" year, six months have thirty days and six months have twenty-nine days. These "full" and "short" months rotate; Nissan is always thirty days, the second month (Iyar) is always twenty-nine, the third month (Sivan) always thirty, etc. For a technical reason, whenever a month has thirty days, two days are celebrated as the head (*rosh hodesh*) of the following month, the thirtieth of the outgoing month and the first of the new month. In months of twenty-nine days, only the first day of the new month is so celebrated.

When the set calendar was established in the third century, intercalation was achieved by adding an extra thirty-day month to the year seven times every nineteen years, given that the number of days in nineteen solar years is extremely close to the number of days in 235 lunar months (12 x 19 + 7), both comprising about 6939.6 days. Rounding out slightly, the relevant equations are:

365.2422 days per year x 19 years = 6939.60 days
29.5305 days per month x 235 months = 6939.67 days

Additional calendrical considerations have necessitated "short years," comprising one day less than the "regular" year, and "complete" years, comprising one day more than the "regular" year. In "short" years, the eighth and ninth months (Ḥeshvan and Kislev) will each have twenty-nine days while in long years each will have thirty days.

4. The Tenth Plague

The proclamation concerning the first month is taught between the announcement of the upcoming tenth plague – the smiting of the Egyptian firstborn – and its fulfillment. Unlike the first nine plagues, the Israelites had to make preparations for the pivotal tenth plague and it was necessary to refer to specific dates of the month.

The final plague was of a totally different order than the first nine, each of which appears to have had parallels, albeit of vastly lesser intensity, in natural phenomena that periodically occur in Egypt. The unprecedented tenth plague – if it had precedence it is only in the sense of parents' sacrificing a child, particularly the firstborn, to their idolatries in times of extraordinary distress – alludes to the profound concept of Hashem exacting judgment against the polytheistic beliefs of Egypt. In the ancient world, the firstborn were often dedicated to the service of the society's gods, surrogates of the priests and signifiers of the deities. Thus, when Hashem informed Moshe and Aharon that He will pass through Egypt on the night of Passover He linked the two, stating He will "strike down every firstborn...and mete out punishments to all the gods of Egypt, I the Lord" (Exod. 12:12). In Numbers 33:4, when describing Israel's leaving Egypt, the Torah states: "The Egyptians were burying those among them whom Hashem struck down, the firstborn, whereby Hashem executed judgment on their gods."

Before the tenth plague occurred the Israelites had to disconnect themselves from their attachment to those idolatrous Egyptian beliefs and express their dedication to

Hashem. Thus, the second subject legislated between the ninth and tenth plagues is the *Pesaḥ* sacrifice.

Each family had to take a lamb or goat on the tenth of the month, protect it from blemish until the fourteenth, at which time it was to be slaughtered to Hashem. The fourteen days between the first of the month when the instructions were given and the sacrifice, especially the interval between the tenth and fourteenth, served as a period of significant spiritual growth for the Israelites and a critical form of preparation for the Exodus. The Egyptians considered these animals sacred, representative of their gods. When Pharaoh had previously agreed to allow Israel to sacrifice but not depart the metropolitan area, Moshe told him: "If we sacrifice the abomination of Egypt before their eyes, will they not stone us!" (Exod. 8:22). The Israelites must have felt tremendous trepidation during those days but surely experienced an enormous change in outlook toward idolatry. The incipient nation had to publicly defy the prevalent pagan beliefs of their mighty human masters and of the society they lived in – beliefs to which many of them were deeply attached (see Josh. 24:14; Ezek. 20:8) – as a necessary condition to the final step in their redemption.

5. Educating the Children

The Covenant that Israel contracted with G-d is of a permanent nature. Israel was conceived to be a corporate entity that would extend through the generations and the inclusion of children was a most critical component. Consequently, parents had a major responsibility to educate their children in Covenant essentials, particularly the details associated with the Exodus and the Lawgiving.

Regarding the latter, Moshe stated: "And you shall make them known to your children and to your children's children, the day you stood before Hashem your G-d at Horeb, when Hashem said to me, 'Assemble the people to

Me that I may have them hear My words so that they learn to revere Me…and their children they shall teach'" (Deut. 4:9-10). Shortly after reviewing the Decalogue, referring to its principles, Moshe stated: וְשִׁנַּנְתָּם לְבָנֶיךָ ("continually repeat them to your children" [6:7]) and וְלִמַּדְתֶּם אֹתָם אֶת בְּנֵיכֶם לְדַבֵּר בָּם ("teach them to your children [such] that they shall speak in them" [11:19]). Children were a key part of the septennial *haqhel* reaffirmation of the Covenant (31:13).

Parents were also required to transmit the fundamental details of the Exodus to their children. A highlight of the annual Passover festival celebration – indeed, a detail established as central to the s*eder* – is, וְהִגַּדְתָּ לְבִנְךָ בַּיּוֹם הַהוּא לֵאמֹר בַּעֲבוּר זֶה וְגוֹ' ("And you shall relate to your son on that day, saying, 'for this purpose Hashem did for me what He did in my departing Egypt'" [Exod. 13:8]).*[2] Parents are instructed to recount to their children not merely the events that occurred but also G-d's purpose of the redemption. This connects with the story of the Covenant and the Lawgiving.

In three different contexts (Exod. 12:26; 13:14; Deut. 6:20) the Torah speaks of a son who asks a question to his father concerning an aspect of the Passover commemoration. In a fourth context, the father is bidden to teach his son about the Passover details without the mention of a question (Exod. 13:8). The formulators of the Passover Haggadah (based on the Mekhilta [*Parashat Bo* 18]) composed a homily utilizing these passages to alert parents to a critically important concept concerning educating their children. "The Torah speaks in accordance with four [types of] sons: One is wise, one is wicked, one is simple and one doesn't know how to ask." Each of the three who asks a question is presumed to ask a different

---

[2] For a fuller discussion on this topic see our study *On Exodus Chapter 13* (available at www.Judaic.org).

question and the approach to each son is different. What may succeed with one may not succeed with another. חֲנֹךְ לַנַּעַר עַל פִּי דַרְכּוֹ ("Educate the youth according to his tendencies") גַּם כִּי יַזְקִין לֹא יָסוּר מִמֶּנָּה ("even when he grows old he will not swerve from it" [Prov. 22:6]).

The Korban Pesah and the Repudiation of Avodah Zarah

Dr. Moshe Sokolow

The principle objective of this essay is to explain the significance of the original *korban pesah* as a repudiation of idolatry and a demonstration of complete faith in God. Along the way we will also seek to clarify some of the laws of the *korban pesah* (as detailed in Exodus 12), as well as some passages in the Haggadah. The material is presented in the form of questions and answers, much like the Haggadah itself.

I. The "Wicked" Son: Why is Exclusion an Act of Heresy?

The wicked son asks: מה העבודה הזאת לכם?, "What is this ritual to you?" The Haggadah replies: לכם ולא לו, ולפי שהוציא את עצמו מן הכלל—כפר בעיקר, "[His use of the word] 'You' excludes himself. Since he has excluded himself from the general rule, he has rejected an article [of faith]."

Question:
Why is the refusal to participate in the *korban pesah* regarded as a rejection of faith, an act of heresy? If someone fails to observe Shabbat, Kashrut, or Yom haKippurim, we don't necessarily declare them to be heretics. Why is Pesah different?

Information to Consider:
After the plague of *arov*, Pharaoh offered to allow the Jews to bring sacrifices to God without leaving Egypt. Moshe declines the offer, explaining (Exodus 8:22):

ויאמר משה לא נכון לעשות כן כי תועבת מצרים נזבח ליקוק
אלקינו הן נזבח את תועבת מצרים לעיניהם ולא יסקלנו :

It would not be proper because the Egyptians regard
our sacrifices to the LORD as abominations. Could
we break an Egyptian taboo [תועבת מצרים] before
their very eyes without getting stoned?

[**Note**: We may recall that because the Egyptians held the eaters
of the flesh of sheep and cattle in the lowest regard, Joseph's
brothers were fed separately from the other Egyptians (Gen.
43:32). Joseph also encouraged his brothers to list their
occupations as shepherds in order to keep them isolated from the
rest of Egypt (46:34). Both of these references feature the word
תועבה.]

Answer:

1. To slaughter and eat the *korban pesah* in public was to
   offer the gravest insult to the Egyptians and to their
   gods. Only those Israelites who were firmly committed
   to God and to Moshe were prepared to take that risk. To
   participate under those circumstances was an instance
   of *mesirut nefesh* of total dedication. To refuse to
   participate meant that one was not convinced that God
   could really do all that He had promised, and that one
   still feared the Egyptians more than one feared God.

2. While a transgression of Shabbat or of kashrut is
   regrettable, it does not, per se, constitute either a denial
   of God or the recognition of some other power as
   greater than His. To reject the *korban pesah*, however,
   is to reject monotheism in its struggle for recognition
   over the "abominations" of idolatry.

3. The self-exclusion of the "wicked" son from this ritual
   is tantamount to his refusal to disavow idolatry. The
   Haggadah's observation: "Were he there [in Egypt] he
   would not have been redeemed," is self-explanatory. By

rejecting the *korban pesah*– by honoring Egyptian abomination over divine commandment– he forfeited his right to redemption.

II. Preparation of the Korban Pesah in Exodus Ch. 12

Question #1:

Why was the 15th of Nisan chosen for the *korban*?

Why was it necessary to select the sacrificial animal on the 10th day of Nisan?

Why was the blood smeared on the door-posts and lintel?

Answer:

The challenge of the *korban pesah*, as we have just explained, was to see if the Jews would stake their lives on God and Moshe, and free themselves from their subservience to, and fear of, the Egyptians. Anything that increased the indignity to the Egyptians heightened the risk to the Jews and made the test more meaningful.

Bearing this in mind, we can appreciate why the 15th of Nisan was chosen for the *korban*: The astrological symbol of the month of Nisan is Aries, the ram, and the 15th day is the climax of a lunar month. The god of the Egyptians was to be slaughtered on the evening of the full moon of its very own month (ostensibly, the height of its own powers), and the Egyptians would be powerless to prevent it! By selecting the sheep or ram four days in advance of the actual sacrifice, the Jews were flaunting their intentions in the faces of their Egyptian neighbors, as though daring them to interfere.

Similarly, the requirement that its blood be smeared on the door-posts and lintel was intended to force them to suffer the further indignity of seeing the lifeblood of the animal, the essence of many pagan rituals, "profaned." While the Torah doesn't specifically say so, we assume that the blood was smeared on the *outside* of the doorposts and lintel to mark the house as a participant in the ritual and eligible, thereby, for protection from the plague.

Question #2:

Why is it forbidden to eat the *korban pesah* raw [נא]?
Why can it not be cooked in a pot [מבושל באש] but only roasted [צלי-אש]?
Why did it have to be roasted whole [-ראשו על-כרעיו ועל קרבו] with its head, hind parts, and internal organs, intact?

Answer:

These details (vs. 9) were intended to increase the indignity the Egyptians were meant to suffer--and, correspondingly, increase the risk to the Jews participating in the sacrifice.

Roasting the sheep (or ram), rather than cooking it in a pot or eating it raw, meant that the aroma could not be contained. Even if the Egyptians did not actually see their taboo being slaughtered, they could not avoid the smell. By requiring the principal organs to be kept intact, the identity of the roasting animal could not be denied.

A Jew, who had slaughtered his *korban pesah* secretly, still fearing Egyptian reprisals, could not easily disguise its subsequent preparation. His participation in the ritual of redemption had to be made public, one way or another.

These same points are made by a commentary to the Torah, *Da'at Zekenim miBa'alei haTosafot*:

[פי' ראבי"ע]
דלפי שתועבת מצרים תזבחו, שמא תאמרו לא נצלהו כל צרכו פן ירגישו בו המצרים! ת"ל אל תאכלו ממנו נא.
ושמא תאמרו נבשלנו ונכסנו בקדרה, ת"ל ובשל מבושל.
ושמא תאמרו לחתוך הראש והכרעים ואל יכירו מה זאת, ת"ל ראשו על כרעיו ועל קרבו.

106

[Rabbi Avraham ben Ezra explained:]
Since you are about to sacrifice an Egyptian abomination you might not think to roast it entirely, lest the Egyptians realize it. Therefore it says, "Do not eat any of it raw."

Since you might think to cook it in a closed pot, it says, "[Do not eat any of it...] cooked"

And lest you think to cut off its head or legs so they can't tell what it is, it says, "[roasted-] head, legs, and entrails."

III. Participation in the Sacrificial Meal

Question #1:

What is a *ben neikhar* (v. 43) and why is he prohibited to eat the *korban pesah*?

Answer:

Since the entire purpose of *the korban pesah* was to force the Jews to relinquish their fears of the Egyptians and declare their allegiance to God, it is obvious that non-Jews could not participate. Assuming, then, that the Torah is not merely stating the obvious, whom does it mean to exclude? Targum Onkelos's translation reflects this concern. He translates *ben neikhar* as: בר ישראל דאסתלק, "a Jew who has removed himself." This interpretation fits neatly into our own analysis of the "wicked son," who had also "removed himself" from the *korban pesah*. It is also reflected in Rashi's commentary: שנתכרו מעשיו לאביו שבשמים, "one whose actions have alienated him from God."

Question #2:

Why is someone who is uncircumcised [*areil*] forbidden to partake of it (v. 48)?

Answer:

Regarding the exclusion of the *areil* from the *korban pesah*, we note that Yehoshua was commanded to circumcise all the Jews who were not circumcised in the desert, before they could participate in the first *korban pesah* to be celebrated in Eretz Yisrael (Joshua 5:2 ff.). One phrase which occurs there, and which duplicates a phrase we cited in the first section, gives us a clue about the relationship of *berit milah* to the *korban pesah*.

The phrase in Joshua (5:9) is: היום גלותי את-חרפת מצרים מעליכם; "Today, I [God] have removed the disgrace of Egypt from upon you." On the analogy of תועבת מצרים, the abomination of Egypt, which described their taboos of sacrificing or eating sheep (Gen. 43:32, 46:34, and Exodus 8:22), we have a reference, here, to the scorn which the Egyptians apparently heaped upon the Jewish ritual of circumcision.

Just as someone who has not broken completely with idolatry and its taboos is excluded from the *korban pesah*— because it symbolizes total belief in God—so do we exclude someone whose sensitivity to the scorn of idolaters prevents him from undergoing circumcision. If a gentile slave or a resident alien [גר תושב] undergoes circumcision, however, he becomes eligible to participate on an equal footing with a Jew (Exodus 12:44, 48).

Question #3:

Was circumcision a prerequisite for the original *korban pesah* too?

Answer:

Reason dictates that circumcision, like the repudiation of idolatry, was a necessary prerequisite for the redemption from Egypt and, hence, for participation in the original *korban pesah*. The problem is that there does not appear to be an explicit reference to this in the Torah.

Two later verses, however, and one Midrash, fill in this gap. First of all, the verse we cited above (Joshua 5:2) instructed him "to circumcise the Israelites a second time"

[שנית]. If this was to be the second time, when was the first? A subsequent verse (5) answers: "All the people who came out [of Egypt] had been circumcised," suggesting that a similar mass circumcision had taken place prior to the Exodus! [The use, here, of the passive participle, מולים היו, as opposed to the verbal passive, נמולו (cf. Gen. 17:27), also indicates that their state of being circumcised was intentional.]

A similar conclusion can be drawn from a prophecy of Yehezkel concerning Yerushalayim (chapter 16). Describing Israel, metaphorically, as a newborn infant abandoned in the field by its parents [as Israelite parents, according to an Aggadah, actually did with their offspring in Egypt], God says (v. 16):

ואעבור עליך ואראך מתבוססת בדמיך. ואומר לך בדמיך חיי,
ואומר לך בדמיך חיי:

I passed by and saw you wallowing in your own blood, and I said to you, 'In your blood, live'! I said to you, 'In your blood, live'!

To what blood does this refer? A Midrash replies (*Shemot Rabbah* 17:3):

מה ראה הקב״ה להגן עליהם בדם כדי לזכור להם דם מילת
אברהם, ובב׳ דמים ניצולו ישראל ממצרים בדם פסח ובדם
מילה.

Why did God see fit to protect them by means of blood [on the doorposts]? To remind them of the blood of Abraham's circumcision. Israel was rescued from Egypt by virtue of two types of blood: The blood of [*Korban*] *Pesah*, and the blood of circumcision.

A trace of this Midrashic tradition can still be found in those versions of the Haggadah which, following the custom of the AR"I, include the verse from Ezekiel 16:6 in a Midrashic homily on Devarim 26:5, ויהי-שם לגוי גדול עצום ורב.

IV. Conclusion

The Exodus from Egypt figures very prominently throughout the Torah. Many mitzvot are linked to the Exodus, demonstrating its centrality to Jewish law and lore. In this essay we have endeavored to demonstrate just how central the original Pesah sacrifice (known by the Talmud as *pesah mitzrayim*) was to the experience of freedom and deliverance, and why its annual observance remains such an indispensable feature of Jewish life.

The Nine Aspects of the Haggada[1]

Rabbi Joseph B. Soloveitchik

The Haggada is based upon and revolves around the section in the Torah known as the *"Arami Oved Avi"* portion, which appears at the beginning of *Sidrat Ki Tavo* (*Devarim* 26). This is the passage that each Jew recited upon bringing the first fruits, the *Bikkurim*, to the Temple in Jerusalem. It is clear from the Talmud in *Pesaḥim* 116a, and the Rambam's codification in *Hilkhot Ḥametz u'Matza* (7:1, 7:4), that the recitation of this passage is essential to the fulfillment of the *Mitzva* of *Sippur Yetziat Mitzrayim*. Why in fact do our sages choose this passage as the focal point of the Haggada?

We must conclude that each Jew, in addition to offering the first fruits, was commanded to fulfill the *Mitzva* of *Sippur Yetziat Mitzrayim*. Thus there are two times during the year that the Jew must relate the story of the Exodus from Egypt; at the *Hava'at Bikkurim* and on the night of the Seder.

The Torah presented us with the text for the *Hava'at Bikkurim*. However, with regards to the Seder night all that we find in the Torah is the general commandment: "You shall tell your son on that day, saying, this is done (the *Pesaḥ* observance) because of what the Eternal did for me when I came out of Egypt" (*Shemot* 13:8). A specific text is not mandated. *ḤaZa"L*, however, concluded that the *"Arami Oved Avi"* text which fulfilled the requirement of *Sippur* at the bringing of the *Bikkurim* would also be appropriate at the Seder.

The use of a common text indicates that the seemingly distinct rituals, in fact, have a common theme or purpose. That purpose is to give thanks and express gratitude to the

---

[1] Reprinted with permission from *The Yeshiva University Haggada* (Student Organization of Yeshiva, 1985).

Almighty. Both recitations are acts of *Hakkarat haTov* to the Eternal.

The essence of the Seder, and hence that of *Sippur Yetziat Mitzrayim*, is the expression of gratitude to the Almighty on the great liberation and miracles that he wrought for us in Egypt. As the Rambam states in *Sefer haMitzvot*: "We are commanded to tell the story at the beginning of the fifteenth of Nisan...and we are to thank Him for all the goodness He has bestowed upon us" (*Mitzva* 157). On the Seder night at the climax of *Maggid* we say: "Therefore we are obligated to thank and praise... exalt and revere Him who performed all those miracles and for us."

Similarly, the act of *Hava'at Bikkurim* is an expression of thanksgiving and gratitude to the Almighty for granting the farmer and the people this holy land and its abundance after a history of wandering and suffering. The Jew recognizes that this land has come to him and his nation through a chain of miraculous and divinely ordained episodes throughout history. Therefore, the *Arami Oved Avi* passage contains a short synopsis of early history, with an emphasis on the enslavement in Egypt, the Exodus and the entry into the Land of Israel. The Jew, when bringing the *Bikkurim* states (*Devarim* 26:3): "I say today before the Lord, your God..." However, the *Targum* of *Yonatan Ben Uziel* translates: "I will give gratitude and praise this day to the Lord..." The passage was understood by *HaZa"L* as a statement of thanksgiving and gratitude to the Almighty. (In fact, from this comment of the Targum it is possible to suggest that the word Haggada does not only imply the idea of "telling," but also the notion of thanksgiving and gratitude.)

1) Let us now analyze some of the various aspects of the Haggada. It will help us to begin with a comparison of the *Sippur Yetziat Mitzrayim* that the Jew engages in at the *Hava'at haBikkurim* and that of the Seder night. The

common feature and first aspect of *Sippur Yetziat Mitzrayim* on both these occasions is the *Sippur*. We read and tell a story. This recitation must consist of the biblical text of the *Arami Oved Avi* passage. In a word, we engage in *Mikra*. In this respect the *Hava'at Bikkurim* and the Seder night are identical.

2) At this stage, however, the two rituals part company. In the act of *Hava'at Bikkurim*, the Torah only required that a text be recited. There is no requirement that it be translated or elaborated upon. In contrast, on the Seder night there are additional demands. The *Mitzva* of *Sippur Yetziat Mitzrayim* at the Seder is basically an act of *Talmud Torah*. *Talmud Torah* involves within it elaboration and exegesis. The *Mishna* in *Pesahim* (10:4) mandates: "And he explains and elaborates from *Arami Oved Avi* until he concludes the whole portion." The Mishna speaks of "*Limud*" which involves translation, asking of questions and conceptualization. In fact, the core of *Maggid* is a systematic exegesis and discussion of every word of the *Arami Oved Avi* passage. We engage in a *Torah she-B'al Peh* analysis of a *Torah she-Bikhtav* text.

This analysis utilizes all the elements that comprise *Torah she-B'al Peh*. For our purposes these elements may be subdivided into three different areas. The first is Midrash. This refers to the exegesis of biblical verses in accordance with the hermeneutical rules set down by our sages (e.g., the Thirteen *Middot* of Rabbi Yishmael, the Thirty-two *Middot* of Rabbi Eliezer).

The second category is *Mishna*. This refers to the set laws and statements cited in the *Mishnayot* and *Memrot*.

Finally, we have *Gemara*, which refers to halakhic analysis and conceptualization. Rashi in various places in the Talmud translates *Gemara* as the *Sevarot*- the logical basis for the laws of the *Mishna*. However, the most full and eloquent definition is given by Rambam in *Hilkhot Talmud Torah* (1:11): "And one is obligated to apportion his time of study, so that he spends one-third of his time studying *Torah she-Bikhtav*, another third studying *Torah she-B'al Peh*, and one-third in understanding and trying to see the development from one step to another from beginning to end, and he should compare cases and derive one idea from another; these elements are called *Gemara*."

In the Haggada we find that all three areas of the oral law are used and applied. Firstly, we have *Midrash*. As was quoted above, the *Arami Oved Avi* passage is interpreted and explained through the different devices of Midrash. Secondly, the Haggada includes a number of passages of *Mishna*, of set halakhot and statements. Examples include the passage taken from the *Mishna* in *Pesahim* (10:5) "Rabban Gamliel used to say, anyone who has not said these three things at Passover has not fulfilled his obligation, etc.," and the response to the wise son "And you shall even tell him, (all the halakhot including) 'We do not eat any food after the eating of the Afikoman'," which is a law found in the *Mishna* in *Pesahim* (10:8). Finally, the Haggada contains elements of "*Gemara*," of logical deductions and inferences. An example of this is the passage "Therefore, it is our duty to thank, praise…" which is a logical conclusion based upon the reading of the immediately preceding halakhot (i.e., *Pesah*, *Matzah* and *Maror*). Thus the Haggada not only involves *Mikra*, but also *Limud*. In fact the word Haggada and its root "*Haged*" imply not only telling, but also an act of study and *Talmud Torah*, as we find prior to *Matan Torah* when the Almighty commands Moshe, "Thus shall you say to the House of Yaakov and tell (*vetagged*) to the Children of Israel" (*Shemot* 19:3).

3) It is not enough, however, for the Jew to be a student the night of the Seder; he must also become a teacher. This reflects the third aspect of the Haggada—*Masora*. The Jew must teach his children and others about the glorious event that occurred in Egypt long ago. The Haggada, before the

passage about the four sons, included the portion "Blessed be the Omnipotent. Blessed be He who hath given the Torah to his people Israel. Blessed be He, etc." What, in fact, is this passage? In a word, it is a short version of *Birkat haTorah* – the blessing made on the Torah. If we carefully examine the Torah blessings, in general, we see that they, too, stress the aspect of *Masora*, the passing on of tradition. We state "And the house of Israel. And we and our children and our children's children should all be privileged to know your name, and be students of your Torah for its own sake." Moreover, at the close of the blessing we say, "Blessed be the Lord, who teaches Torah to His people, Israel." It is as if the Almighty himself becomes part of that *Masora* community. After this blessing, appears the passage about the four sons, which concretizes the notion of teaching and passing on the story of the Exodus to one's children, each at his respective level.

4) The fourth aspect is the "question and answer" style dialogue that is found in parts of the Haggada. Why is it so crucial that the child ask questions; why do we prompt him? Simply put, Judaism insists that God reveals himself to the man who seeks after and thirsts for God. The verse in *Devarim* (4:29) reads: "But if you search there for the Lord your God, you will find him if only you will seek him with all your heart and soul." We want to initiate the child into the *Masora* community that seeks out the Almighty and yearns for his presence and illumination. We want the child to become a "*Mevakesh Hashem*"—"a seeker of God."

5) The fifth aspect of *Sippur Yetziat Mitzrayim* is the central role that the meal and food play at the Seder. The drama of *Sippur Yetziat Mitzrayim* begins with Kiddush and closes with *Nishmat* and *Yishtabah* after the meal. In fact, this is the reason that the *Shulhan Arukh* (*Orah Hayyim* 472:1) is so careful in specifying that the Kiddush on the night of the fifteenth of Nisan should be recited after

astronomical nightfall. (On other festivals, one may usher in the festival and recite Kiddush earlier when it is still daytime.) Kiddush is part of *Sippur Yetziat Mitzrayim*, and therefore, must take place on the night of the fifteenth proper. Kiddush the night of *Pesah* plays two roles. One is the normal role of Kiddush as the introduction of the festive meal as on every festival. Secondly, it is part of *Sippur Yetziat Mitzrayim*. Kiddush contains within it the statement "who has chosen us from all nations," which is identical to the third language of *Ge'ulat Mitzrayim* found in *Sidrat Va'era* (*Shemot* 6:7): "*Velakaḥti*"—"and shall take you unto me for a nation."

Moreover, there is another more basic reason for Kiddush playing a role in *Sippur Yetziat Mitzrayim*. *Sippur Yetziat Mitzrayim* contains within it two elements. One is the recitation of certain passages. Second, is the element of performing certain actions, eating of certain foods, etc. When one eats Matzah, Maror, and Korban Pesah on the Seder night one fulfills these specific *mitzvot*. However, in addition, through the eating of these foods one is able to teach and convey the messages of *Ge'ulat Mitzrayim*. They function as audio-visual aids in our educational scheme, namely, the Seder. This is what Rabban Gamliel was trying to convey (in the *Mishna* [*Pesahim* 10:5] "Whoever has not said these three things has not fulfilled his obligation, etc."). He wanted the Jew, before he partakes of the foods, to explain their significance and message to all who are at this table. *Sippur Yetziat Mizrayim* is a careful blend, then, of narrative, teaching and actions to get across a unified message.

Kiddush also opens the *Seuda* every Shabbat and festival. Kiddush puts the meal in a context of holiness, uplifting it from a mundane effort to satisfy biological needs to the realm of the sacred. The idea of "a meal before God" is a fundamental one in Judaism.

It is along these lines that our sages (*Berakhot* 55a) spoke of "an individual's table is an atonement for his sins" and "a dining table is similar to an altar."

6) As was previously stated, the *Mikra Bikkurim* involves praise and thanksgiving to the Almighty. However, this is an awareness that comes about indirectly. The farmer recites the *Arami Oved Avi* passage which in itself, when understood, expresses gratitude. It is almost a notion of "*K'riyata zu Hilula*" (Megillah 14a). The praise is implicit in the narration. In contrast, on the night of the Seder we are enjoined not only to praise and give gratitude, but rather to break forth into spontaneous song – "Let us, therefore, sing a new song in his presence, Halleluyah." The Jew's heart is overflowing with feelings of joy and thanksgiving. It is the night of the great romance between the Almighty and *K'nesset Yisrael*– "I am to my beloved and my beloved is to me." It is these feelings that are expressed in the custom of reading the book of *Shir haShirim* the night of the Seder.

Philosophically, one can ask, who is lowly man that he should have the audacity to praise God? Is not man "dust and ashes"? How then does he have the right to praise the infinite being, the Almighty? The halakha responds: True, philosophically there may be problems; however the Jew cannot contain himself. The Jew, on the night of the Seder, is overflowing with thanksgiving and song to God, and he cannot repress this authentic need to express his gratitude to the Holy one, Blessed be He.

7) As the Jew approaches the Story of the Exodus, there may be a tendency to look at the event as remote and distant from the here and now. Therefore, the Haggada contains within it three passages that help us deal with this problem. First of all, before the recitation of the *Arami Oved Avi* passage, we say: "And if God had not taken our ancestors out of Egypt, we and our children and our

117

children's children would still be enslaved in Egypt." We make a declaration of relevance. Why, in fact, are we discussing these events of history; what is their relevance to our present situation? And to this we respond that were it not for the redemption in Egypt, there would be no Jewish People today.

Secondly, before Hallel we recite that "in every generation a person should look upon himself as if he personally had come out of Egypt. Not our ancestors alone did the Holy One, Blessed be He, redeem, but us also He redeemed with them." The events of *Yetziat Mitzrayim* are not only relevant to us; rather, we are actually re-experiencing history on the night of the Seder. It is a current as well as a historical event. This recognition enables us to recite *Hallel* and break forth into spontaneous song, because it is we who left Egypt as well.

Finally, we recite the *"Vehi she'Amda"* passage: "For not only one tyrant has risen up against us to destroy us, but in every generation tyrants have sought to destroy us and the Holy One, Blessed be He, delivered us from their hands." Not only do we relive the experience of Egypt, but we also realize that danger and annihilation threaten the Jewish people in every generation and locale. We move from the historical events to a better understanding of our current situation. The custom is that at this point in the Seder one lifts up his cup of wine. Why is this done? The cup is the symbol of Jewish destiny and eternity- *netzah Yisrael*, as the verse (Psalms 116:13) "A cup of salvation I shall uplift, and call on the Almighty's name" indicates. At the Seder we speak of the relevance of historical events, the reliving of those events and the cycle of danger and redemption that is characteristic of Jewish history.

8) The *Mishna* in *Pesahim* (10:5) dictates "and he explains the *Arami Oved Avi* passage until he completes it." However, in our Haggada we do not complete the passage in its totality. We do not recite and discuss the last verse

and a half, which read: "He hath brought us into this place, and hath given us this land, a land flowing (with) milk and honey. And now, behold, I have brought the first of the fruits of the land which Thou hast given to me, O Lord…" (Deuteronomy 26:9-10). The farmer bringing the *bikkurim* would include these verses and then set down the fruits "before the Lord your God." It is understandable why the Haggada did not include the last verse that discusses the actual bringing of fruits, as that is out of place on the Seder night. However, why was the verse discussing the entry into the Land of Israel not included in our version of the Haggada? A number of approaches exist to resolve this problem.

First of all, if we included this reference to the Land of Israel, we would convey the impression that there are five expressions of or references to *Ge'ula* and not four (as we maintain). We would include "*veheveti*" as one of the references to *Ge'ula*, and *ḤaZa"L* felt that this would not be appropriate on the Seder night. Why is this the case? Firstly, the four references to *Ge'ula* that were stated by the Almighty to Moshe in *Sidrat Va'era* were new ideas that had not been expressed to the Patriarchs. However, "*veheveti*," "and I shall bring you into the land…" was already promised to Avraham, Yitzhak, and Ya'akov individually in the *B'rit Avot*. They were already promised that their descendants would inherit the Land of Israel. Secondly, although the Jewish people did enter into the Land of Israel subsequent to the Exodus from Egypt, this was not the primary goal of *Yetziat Mitzrayim*. It was their destination but not their destiny. The direct goal of *Yetziat Mitzrayim* was the revelation at Sinai. The goal was the transformation of a subjugated people into "a nation of priests and a holy nation." It was not just to grant them political and economic freedom, but also to create a sacred people. Moshe, at the episode of the burning bush, asked the Almighty: "Who (am) I that I should go unto Pharaoh,

119

and that I should bring forth the Children of Israel out of Egypt?" (Exodus 3:11). And the Almighty gives an answer that seems at first to be a bit difficult: "Certainly I will be with you and this shall be unto you the sign that I have sent you: When thou has brought forth the people out of Egypt they shall serve God upon this mountain." What was the Almighty saying to Moshe; how did this answer his query? The Almighty was stating: Know, Moshe, that the purpose of *Ge'ulat Mitzrayim* is not political and social freedom. For that task, I would not have picked you. I did not pick you to be a diplomat or a king or political leader. Rather, the purpose of the Exodus is to create a holy nation, to make them a Torah nation. For this purpose, God says, I need a Rebbe, a teacher and mentor who will lead and guide this people. And for this role, you are the best candidate. *Pesaḥ* is the holiday of *Yetziat Mitzrayim* and leads into Shavuot and *Matan Torah*. These two festivals do not focus on the Land of Israel as a central theme. According to Rambam in *Moreh Nevukhim* (3:43), it is instead Sukkot that celebrates the Land of Israel.

Thirdly, it is possible to suggest that during the time the Temple still stood, the text of the Haggada did include the last verses relating to the entry into the Land of Israel. Upon the destruction of the Temple and the subsequent exile, *ḤaZa"L* amended the text in order to conform to the new reality in which *Am Yisrael* found itself.

9) Finally, on the night of the Seder, the Jew mentions all the wonderful things that the Almighty has done and is doing for him and his people. This, in fact, is the thrust of *Birkat haMazon* and, therefore, it also functions as part of *Sippur Yetziat Mitzrayim* (in addition to its role as grace after the meal.) After discussing God's special relationship with the Jewish People we move to the *Hallel haGadol*, which contains a recognition of God's benevolence to the whole world. We recognize and express gratitude for this, as we state, "Who giveth food unto all flesh, for His

kindness endures forever." This leads us to the climax of the Seder, "*Nishmat*," when we speak of the future, the *Aharit haYamim*, when all living beings shall give praise to the Almighty – "*Nishmat kol ḥai tevarekh...*" These portions add a glorious eschatological dimension to the *Shevach* and *Hoda'a* sections that are so essential to the Haggada.

Encourage Questioning[1]

Rabbi Ralph Tawil

Value: Encourage questioning.
Questions are the way that we seek information from the world. It is an important aspect of an aware and cognizant approach to the world. Questioning takes courage; it means being able to admit that you are seeking information that you do not know. This admission can be hard for some and therefore some are embarrassed to ask. Our sages have taught us that "the bashful pupil cannot learn." For the same reason, the "quick-to-anger teacher cannot teach." Real teaching and learning must include a free and open dialogue between the students and their teacher. Just as much as it is the teacher's obligation to teach when we see that our students do not understand, it is the student's obligation to ask when something is unclear. As parents, our obligation is even greater. We are our children's primary source of knowledge about the world. We must take the time to explain carefully, to probe their understanding, and most importantly to encourage questioning.

Text: Masekhet Pesahim (p. 116a)
The text that defines the Pesah Seder is the Haggadah. The Mishna and Talmud in the tenth chapter of Masekhet Pesahim record the guidelines for conducting the Seder.

> Mishna: The second cup is mixed (poured), and here the child asks. And if the child doesn't know to ask, the parent teaches him—how different is this night (*Ma Nishtana*) from all the other nights...

---

[1] The following is from Rabbi Tawil's Table Talks for Pesah (Lesson 1).

Gemara: If the child is wise—he asks. If he is not—his wife asks. If not—he should ask himself. Even two sages who know the laws of Pesah ask one another.

Analysis

Asking is the mainstay of the evening. The parents do things that would arouse the children's questions, like removing the tray (table) before the meal, breaking the massah, etc. If the child does not ask, then the parent has to encourage the child to notice the unusual aspects of the evening in order to ask questions. (According to this understanding, the *Ma Nishtana* questions are not the questions that the children ask, but the way the parent encourages his children to observe the unusual aspects of the evening. But let your young children recite it anyway—they worked so hard to learn it!).

Interestingly, a person who is alone for the Seder must ask himself questions. Questions are a way of seeking knowledge. The person who has no one to ask him questions must still find new questions to ask. This rabbinic directive encourages everyone, no matter how learned, to explore the exodus from Egypt anew in order to seek more information from it, thereby deepening and renewing our understanding of these miraculous events.

Therefore, in addition to the reciting of the *Ma Nishtana*, encourage your children to ask other questions. Rambam, based on the Talmud, advises:

> One must make a change in the routine on this night so that the children will take note and ask, and say, "How different this night is from all other nights!" and the father will answer them and say to them "such and such happened, such and such took place." How does one make a change? By distributing parched corn or nuts, or by removing the table before them before they eat, or by snatching things from one another's hands, and similar things. (*Mishneh Torah, Hilkhot Hames u'Massah* 7:3)

Giving candy (parched corn and nuts) at the beginning of the meal, along with the other practices, are meant to break the routine—to encourage the children to notice the difference. Other things can be done to create surprise and difference (Idea: ask your adult guests to think up some unusual things to do. See below for some ideas.) Of course, the best way is by asking your own new questions about Pesah.

Ideas of how to stimulate questions: 1) place unusual items around the seder table that are connected to the haggadah and have the children match the item with the appropriate part of the seder. For example, put a clock set to midnight—when Hashem began to kill the firstborn; place a card that has the mathematical examples 5 x 10, 5 x 40, 5 x 50 (this represents the derasha about how many plagues happened at the splitting of the sea), and other ideas. 2) Have a "jeopardy" kind of game, where you give the answer and the child supplies the question. For example, "when we eat this seder item we do not recline"—"What is Marror?" 3) Pack suitcases for the journey out of Egypt.

The following letter to the editor about the importance of questions appeared in the *New York Times* (January 19, 1988, by Donald Sheff):

To the Editor:
Isidor I. Rabi, the Nobel laureate in physics was once asked, "Why did you become a scientist, rather than a doctor or lawyer or businessman, like the other immigrant kids in your neighborhood?"
"My mother made me a scientist without ever intending it. Every other Jewish mother in Brooklyn would ask her child after school: 'Nu? Did you learn anything today?' But not my mother. She always asked

124

me a different question. 'Izzy,' she would say, 'did you ask a good question today?' That difference – asking good questions – made me become a scientist.

(The source of this letter and other ideas contained in this article is an excellent haggadah *A Different Night, The Family Participation Haggadah* by Noam Zion and David Dishon [Shalom Hartman Institute, 1997]. I recommend *The Leader's Guide* to this haggadah as well.)